Herbert C. Hoover

31st President of the United States

Herbert C. Hoover was hailed as a hero for his relief work on behalf of the starving Belgian people during World War I and condemned as a villain when he opposed direct federal aid for starving Americans during the Great Depression. He left the presidency wounded and embittered by his country's rejection of him in the 1932 presidential campaign. (Herbert Hoover Presidential Library.)

Herbert C. Hoover

31st President of the United States

Barbara G. Polikoff

 GARRETT EDUCATIONAL CORPORATION

Manufactured in the United States of America

Edited and produced by Synthegraphics Corporation

Library of Congress Cataloging in Publication Data

Polikoff, Barbara Garland.
  Herbert C. Hoover, 31st president of the United States / Barbara Garland Polikoff.
      p.   cm. – (Presidents of the United States)
    Includes bibliographical references.
    Summary: Presents the life of Herbert Hoover, including his childhood, education, employment, and political career.
    1. Hoover, Herbert, 1874–1964–Juvenile literature.
  2. Presidents–United States–Biography–Juvenile literature.   3. United States–Politics and government– 1929–1933–Juvenile literature.   [1. Hoover, Herbert, 1874–1964.   2. Presidents.]   I. Title.   II. Title: Herbert Hoover, thirty-first president of the United States.
  III. Series.
  E802.P67   1990
  973.91'6'092 – dc20
  [B]
  [92]   89-39946
  ISBN 9-944483-58-5   CIP
                                                          AC

Contents

Chronology for Herbert C. Hoover vi

Chapter 1: "Thee Is Going to Oregon" 1

Chapter 2: A Quaker Boyhood 8

Chapter 3: College Years 14

Chapter 4: Three New Suits and a Beard 25

Chapter 5: Assignment in China 34

Chapter 6: "Chief" 41

Chapter 7: "The Slippery Road of Public Life" 48

Chapter 8: The Food King 58

Chapter 9: "Turning Off the Lights" 67

Chapter 10: The Magic Wears Off 79

Chapter 11: A Nation in Despair 89

Chapter 12: "The Heart of a President" 101

Chapter 13: "He Has Endured" 105

Bibliography 117

Index 119

Chronology for
Herbert C. Hoover

1874	Born on August 10 in West Branch, Iowa
1891–1895	Attended Stanford University
1896–1898	Served on various assignments as a mining engineer in California, Colorado, New Mexico, and Australia
1899	Married Lou Henry on February 10 in Monterey, California
1908	Started his own mining consulting firm
1914–1917	Directed the American Relief Committee, then the Commission for Relief in Belgium
1917	Appointed U.S. Food Administrator by President Wilson
1919	Appointed director of the American Relief Administration by President Wilson
1920–1928	Appointed secretary of commerce by President Harding; continued in same post through the Coolidge administration
1928	Elected 31st President of the United States
1932	Defeated for re-election by Franklin Delano Roosevelt
1946	At President Truman's request, went to Europe and Asia to study and make recommendations for famine relief
1954	Honored by a joint resolution of Congress on his 80th birthday
1964	Died on October 20

Chapter 1

"Thee Is Going to Oregon"

At night, fear would swoop down on 10-year-old Herbert "Bert" Hoover like a coal-black bird. During the day he'd either be distracted by the scenery whizzing past the window or by all the people crammed into the train as it wound its way toward Oregon. But at night, lying in a hard wooden bunk with the blanket his Aunt Millie had given him pulled up to his chin, it was hard not to think about all the things that scared him.

What would it be like living with Uncle John Minthorn, Aunt Laura, and two girl cousins? What if he didn't like them? Would he ever see his older brother, Tad, and little sister, May, again? West Branch, Iowa, where they had been living with relatives, and Newberg, Oregon, were so far apart!

Then came the hardest question of all, the question that no one was able to answer in a way that comforted him: Why did his mother have to die? Aunt Millie explained that she had worked so hard after his father's sudden death that the Lord decided it was time to give her a rest. But Bert was sure that if the Lord would have asked his mother about it, she never would have left Tad, May, and him alone, no matter how tired she was.

Bert lived the early years of his childhood in this three-room frame house in the small Quaker farming community of West Branch, Iowa. (Herbert Hoover Presidential Library.)

"SEND THE BOY TO US"

Bert tried to chase the bad memories out of his mind by thinking about funny ones instead. He thought of the farm where he was born back in Iowa. He, his cousin George, and his brother Tad had decided to start a circus after seeing one in Iowa City. They had pulled the old white mare, Mollie, out of the pasture, braided her mane, and with Tad as ringmaster, guided her around the ring made by the old threshing machine. George managed to climb up on Mollie and stand on her back, but the moment she started to gallop, he fell off. Tad didn't do any better. Bert had been secretly glad that the two older boys had said he was too little to try.

Suddenly Bert was brought back to the present when a baby started crying in the bunk next to his. He heard its mother trying to comfort it. The train was filled with mothers and fathers and children, crowded in the cars with all their belongings—clothes, books, musical instruments, pots and pans, tools—all going west to a new home, just as he was.

The only belongings Bert had were two dimes in his pocket, the basket of food Aunt Millie had cooked for him, and a half-empty cardboard suitcase with his clothes and two small, framed Quaker prayers his mother had hung in their kitchen. His father, Jesse, had finally earned enough money to move the family from the cramped, three-room house Bert and Tad had been born in to a larger house. But then Jesse died of typhoid fever. All that he had managed to leave for his widow and children was the new house and a $1,000 insurance policy. The two dimes that Aunt Millie gave Bert as she kissed him good-bye at the railroad station were all she could spare.

Bert turned and wound himself tightly in the blanket, trying to keep his feet warm. The mother had begun to sing to her baby. Pretending that she was his own mother, Bert closed his eyes and her soft voice lulled him to sleep.

Uncle John Minthorn

As the Union Pacific sped through the night, carrying Bert to Oregon, Dr. John Minthorn was making his medical rounds in his horse and buggy in the small Quaker community of

Newberg. He was looking forward to the arrival of his young nephew with an excitement his Quaker reserve concealed. His own son had died the year before. He hoped that his sister Huldah's child would help fill the terrible void in their family.

Dr. Minthorn had seen very little of Huldah since she had married the blacksmith, Jesse Hoover, and had gone to live in the Quaker settlement of West Branch, Iowa. Unlike Huldah, a devout Quaker, Minthorn was not a pacifist (one who is opposed to war and fighting). During the Civil War he fought in the Battle of Shiloh and was to advise Bert, "Turn your cheek once, but if he smites you, then punch him."

Restless and something of an adventurer, Minthorn had lived in many places. He had worked on the Underground Railroad to help slaves escape to Canada, as an Indian agent for the government, as head of an Indian school, as a medical doctor, and most recently, was the founder of a small Quaker school, Newberg Academy.

Minthorn had been devoted to Huldah, his gentle, intelligent, resolute sister whose natural eloquence made her a popular preacher in the lonely tracts of Kansas and Iowa. Caught in a winter storm as she was returning from a Quaker meeting, she had contracted pneumonia and had died. Minthorn knew she had always dreamed that her children would receive a good education. In Newberg, young Bert would be able to get such an education at his academy. In turn, Bert would earn his way by feeding the cows and horses, milking, chopping firewood, and clearing forestland.

Minthorn had always felt that Huldah and Jesse were too easy on their children. He had his own strong ideas on how to bring up a responsible, God-fearing boy. Soon after Huldah's death, he sent a note to Allan Hoover's farm, where Bert was staying: "Send the boy to us." The next day Bert was

Bert (center) with his brother Theodore (Tad) and sister Mary (May) shortly before their mother died and the three children were separated. (Herbert Hoover Presidential Library.)

called into the Hoover living room. "Thee is going to Oregon," his uncle said to him.

THE NEW FAMILY

After seven days of traveling, the train finally arrived in Portland, Oregon. As Bert climbed down the high stairs of the railroad car, holding an empty food basket and his suitcase, a man in a wide-brimmed hat and the dark clothes of a Quaker approached him. The man didn't smile as he told Bert that he was his uncle, John Minthorn. Bert felt numb. Everything seemed so unreal. Leaving Tad and May and his relatives at the railroad station back in Iowa, the long train ride across the plains and through the mountains, the mothers cooking on a stove at the back of the train, the iron wheels whirring in his ears at night. And now this big man with the unsmiling face who had met him at the station and was now helping him get aboard a river steamer.

Bert, naturally shy, could only answer yes or no to his uncle's questions as they sat on the hard seat of the boat, traveling the 20 miles down the Willamette River from Portland to Newberg. After a few minutes, Minthorn sat back and the man and boy were silent for the rest of the river trip. Bert was glad to be able to concentrate on the boat ride. It was the first one he had ever taken.

Leaving the steamer at Newberg, the doctor and Bert rode by horse and buggy to the Minthorn family home in the lush Willamette Valley. The scene that greeted Bert as he sat, mute and worried in the buggy, was a cheerful one. He was able to smile as his Aunt Laura hugged him. She and her daughter, Tennie, were cooking pear jam in a great, black iron pot, and the fruity smell made Bert realize that he was starved. Tennie invited him to pick some pears for himself, and Minthorn asked him to bring firewood with him on his return from the orchard.

"The meanest thing a man can do is nothing," Minthorn said, giving Bert the first of hundreds of lessons he was to preach to him in the six years Bert was to live in Newberg.

Bert had never eaten a pear before. It was the sweetest food he had ever tasted. He ate so many that the first night in his new room in his new house with his new family, he was overcome by a paralyzing stomach ache. He promised himself that if he ever felt better again, he would never eat another pear.

Maybe it was worth getting the stomach ache, though. Aunt Laura came up to his room with a dose of peppermint oil and sat with him until he fell asleep.

Chapter 2
A Quaker Boyhood

J esse Hoover's playful spirit was in full swing that tenth day of August, 1874, when his wife broke the suspense of whether she would give birth to a boy or girl. The lustily crying baby was definitely a boy, Herbert Clark Hoover. The happy father ran down the street in West Branch and knocked on a neighbor's window. "We have another General Grant at our house," he called. (General Ulysses S. Grant was in his second term as President at the time.)

As a small boy, Bert Hoover was so serious and shy that Jesse called him his little "stick-in-the-mud." John Minthorn was the last person in the world to bring young Bert "out of the mud." Idle hands were ungodly hands, he said. He routed Bert from bed to feed and groom the horses, milk the cows, and chop firewood before school. After school there were more chores: clearing a tract of forest and keeping the vegetable garden free of weeds.

Though shy, Bert was strong-willed, and he would often chafe at his uncle's demands. He also knew that he had better hide his hot, rebellious feelings and do what his uncle required. Dr. John Minthorn was head of the family and was providing him with a home. Huldah had taught her son to respect his elders and do the job required of him, even if it meant, as it did now, so many hours spent in the barn that Bert felt he couldn't wash the horse smell from his body. Even his pillow smelled like hay.

Herbert C. Hoover, 31st president of the
United States /
30441000160390
Due: 6/24/03 11:59:00 PM

The Brooklyn bridge
30441000065219
Due: 6/24/03 11:59:00 PM

"DO IT WITH THY MIGHT"

Because Minthorn never allowed work to be done on Sundays (called "First Days" by the Quakers), Bert had to double up on his chores on Saturday, leaving little or no time for play. First Days were taken up with attendance at services at the Friends' meetinghouse, then religious school, and then reading in the Bible and other instructive books, usually with Dr. Minthorn. If novels were permitted, they had to have a moral lesson such as showing "the huge danger of Demon Rum."

The happiest times Bert spent with his uncle were on the drives to visit patients. The trips were sometimes long and rough, and the buggy wheels often got stuck hub-deep in the mud. Bert would take turns with his uncle driving the teams. Bumping along, sometimes for hours at a time, Minthorn, not wanting the hours to be wasted, would lecture to Bert on physiology and American history. (Later, Bert was to be grateful for these lectures when he took his college entrance examinations.)

If the weather were calm, the roads not too bad, and the journey long, Minthorn would abandon his teaching role and become a storyteller. Bert listened, enthralled, as his uncle told about his adventures driving teams for the Underground Railroad to help slaves reach freedom in Canada and his brush with death at the Battle of Shiloh. It was hard for Bert to believe that this stern, unsmiling man had run away as a boy and enlisted in the Union Army.

Laura Minthorn was principal of the little, clapboarded, public school Bert went to with his cousin Tennie for the two years before he entered the Quaker academy in Newberg. Besides Tennie, there was her baby sister, Gertrude. Laura Minthorn found little time away from her daughters and school responsibilities to give more than superficial attention to her nephew, who was growing like a weed in the fresh air of New-berg. The lack of family warmth and affection in Bert's life made it even harder for him to put his mother's death out of his mind. And what he wouldn't give to see Tad and May for just one day!

Despite having a fantastic memory, Bert was restless and bored in school. Even when he transferred to the academy, where his uncle taught history and literature, things weren't much better. "Whatsoever thy hand findeth to do, do it with thy might" was the motto inscribed over the main door of the school. Would he ever get away from being preached to?

A Taste of Independence

When he did have some free time, Bert would head for the woods and a fishing pond. His love for the outdoors devel-oped when he had once spent a summer at an uncle's farm on the Osage Indian Reservation in Oklahoma and had played for long, sunlit hours with the Indian children.

One summer, as a change from his usual routine and as a way to earn some money, Bert went to live for two months with a family in the bottomlands north of Newberg. He weeded onions, for which he was paid 50 cents a day and board. The $30 he earned gave him a taste of independence, and at 14 he solemnly promised himself to be self-supporting as quickly as possible.

Reunion with Tad

Late in September of 1887, Bert received news that sent him flying to share it with Elmer Washburn, a new hired farm-hand he had grown to like. His brother, Tad, was going to come to live with the Minthorns! He and Tad would share a room in the academy building that was being fixed up for them.

Tad was 16, and it had become clear to Uncle Davis Hoover, with whom he had been living, that he would never become a farmer. He didn't want to be a student either, but Minthorn gave him no choice. "Thee must go to school, first, last, and always." Though two years older than Bert, Tad was behind in his schooling and entered Bert's class at the academy.

Tad became good friends with Elmer, and the three boys spent many of their free hours together. Only one thing dimmed Bert's pleasure. The first girl he had ever become fond of, Daisy Trueblood, seemed to be more interested in Tad than in him. One night he agonized over a letter which, after much rewriting, he screwed up enough courage to send:

> Friend Daisy,
>
> (and I hope you are more than my friend, although I do not dare to head it that way yet.) You do not know the extent to which I am enthralled, and I am sure that no girl should be allowed such mastery over any person's heart, unless there are such feelings in her own heart. I could not have helped paying my attentions to you, if I had tried and I am sure I did not try very hard. I do think you care. Do you?
>
> Answer this please.
>
> Bert

There is no record of Daisy's answer, but even if she had been softened by Bert's carefully penned letter, the romance would have been short-lived. John Minthorn decided to move the family to nearby Salem, Oregon, and start a real estate company. Bert had just been graduated from the academy, and surprisingly, Minthorn didn't press him to continue his education. Instead, he hired Bert as an office boy at $15 a week.

THE NEW BUSINESSMAN

Minthorn's sternness and rigidity on matters of principle be-
lied the generous man he really was. After completing a house
in Salem for his family, he built another house so that Tad,
Bert, and May—Huldah's three children—could at last live
together again. Grandmother Minthorn, a favorite of Bert's,
came from Iowa to care for the young family. However, Tad
chose to live outside of Newberg and work in a sawmill to
save money for his education.

Salem was a thriving city of over 8,000 people. Minthorn, with his Quaker business partners, Ben Cook and
Charles Moore, held title to over 3,000 acres of pear and prune
orchards that they cut into parcels to sell to settlers pouring
into Salem. "No Hot Nights in Summer—Grass Grows in Winter," Minthorn wrote in the advertising brochure for the new
paradise, Silver Falls. He didn't balk at promising all pur-
chasers an end to cyclones, blizzards, and earthquakes, as
well as no more crop failures, and certainly no grasshoppers
and Hessian flies.

A Walking Dictionary

Bert threw himself into his uncle's real estate business with
a wholeheartedness that delighted Minthorn. Demonstrating
an unexpected bent for salesmanship and publicity, Bert over-
came his persistent shyness and met prospective buyers at
the train depot. Escorting them to Silver Falls, he delivered
a hard-sell speech that even his uncle couldn't better.

For the first time, Bert began to utilize his phenomenal
memory. His employer at the Oregon Land Company, Ben
Cook, who was to launch a "Hoover for President" campaign
30 years later, recalled for reporters that Bert was a "walking
dictionary." Quick as a blink of the eye, he could tell you the

status of every real estate deal, the contents of every letter, and the location of every Land Company document.

Bert was gaining self-confidence and sometimes took charge of matters in unexpected ways. A creditors' meeting in the company's office was dragging on endlessly, and tempers were beginning to grow short when suddenly the lights went out. That brought the meeting to an abrupt halt. After the creditors left, Minthorn and Bert were closing up when Minthorn, detecting a certain gleefulness in Bert's manner, asked, "Did thee turn off the lights?" Bert answered with a smile.

A Taste for the Classics

Ambitious to get ahead, Bert enrolled in night school and studied mathematics and Latin. One day, while poring over his Latin book in the company office, Jane Gray, the town banker's daughter, struck up a conversation with him. A lover of literature, she had made it her special mission to introduce the poorly educated working boys in Salem to good books.

Jane left Bert a copy of Sir Walter Scott's *Ivanhoe*. Bert, caught up in the romantic world of knights and their ladies fair, couldn't put the book down. Jane followed the Scott novel with other classics that Bert devoured hungrily. The Quaker diet of "self-improving" books had starved him. By giving him a taste for the classics, Jane became Bert's great friend. Years later, looking back on her influence on him, he called her "angelic."

A year later, someone else who turned out to be significant in Bert's life walked into the Oregon Land Company office—Roger Brown, a mining engineer from the East Coast. Brown started talking to Bert about engineering, a talk that never really ended.

Chapter 3

College Years

Robert Brown's enthusiasm for engineering was contagious—especially to a receptive mind like Bert's. The prospect of being a mining engineer appealed to a young man seeking a way to challenge the world.

"For a year I mulled over it [engineering]," Hoover wrote in his memoirs, "talking to all who would listen. I haunted the little foundry repair shops of the town. I collected catalogues and information on engineering universities." In his search for information, Bert visited a potential mine in the Cascade Mountains with a mining engineer. The engineer determined, on the basis of studies Bert watched him conduct, that digging a mine there would be a disaster. Bert was fascinated. This was work he'd like to do.

OFF TO COLLEGE

Bert set his mind on applying to a new university in Palo Alto, California, founded by Senator Leland Stanford in memory of his son. He knew that his decision to go to a non-Quaker university would upset his uncle, and Grandmother Minthorn's distress would be hard to bear. But because none of the Quaker universities offered a course in engineering, the only thing he could do was try to win them over. Bert was in luck. The representative of Stanford University who administered the admission test was a well-known Quaker scholar, Dr. Joseph Swain. This eased the family's concern, and they withdrew their opposition.

Taking a Gamble

Bert's small-town education didn't prepare him to compete with better educated city boys applying to the university. He failed the entrance examination when he took it in the spring of 1891. But his eagerness and spunk so impressed Swain that he suggested Bert go to Stanford early in the summer, study with tutors, and retake the examination.

Bert decided to take the gamble. He completed his work at the Oregon Land Company office, packed his two dull-colored suits, his bicycle, his usual giant supply of food, pocketed his fortune of $410, and was on the train platform, ready to leave, an hour before the train's arrival. Now nearly 17 years old, he was tall, tanned, and strong, with a square face and shock of thick hair. He almost had to bend over double to kiss his tiny grandmother good-bye. As she hugged him, her eyes filled with tears. "I think thy mother would like to see thee now," she said.

The First Boarder

Palo Alto, meaning "Tall Tree," was ideally located. To the west were the coastal mountains, and beyond was the Pacific Ocean. Thirty miles north lay cosmopolitan San Francisco. But Palo Alto was too small to have a railroad station, and Bert had to get off at Menlo Park and take a cab to "Stanford Farm," the name given to the campus being built in an old hayfield on Leland Stanford's sprawling estate.

Bert found the campus teeming with carpenters trying to finish a group of one-story buildings for the grand opening of the university on October 1. Piles of lumber and scaffolding blocked his path, the sound of hammers and saws was nearly constant, and sawdust found its way into the morning cereal. But the rawness of the university echoed Bert's own feeling of being untried, and he found the atmosphere so heady it was difficult for him to quiet down enough to sleep those first nights in Room 38 of Encina Hall, where he was the school's first overnight boarder.

A ROUGH BEGINNING

Bert shut out the sounds of the workmen and concentrated on studying for the examinations. As the summer passed and the time for the tests drew near, he had to fight panic. So much was at stake. He passed geometry and algebra with ease, did tolerably well in American history, English, and American literature. His downfall, however, was composition. Because he could not write a decent essay, he failed the test miserably.

Bert was despondent. He pictured himself returning, defeated, to Salem. Were all his dreams of becoming an engineer to be doomed because he failed one test? Fortunately, Bert was allowed a "condition" in English. This meant that he would be admitted to Stanford but would not be able to graduate in 1895 unless he passed the composition test before then.

Bert's sense of relief was not to be long-lived, however. Somehow, he had miscounted the number of required entrance exam subjects he needed and was one short. And he had only one day to prepare for the taking of that needed examination! Relying upon all those lectures Dr. Minthorn had given him as they bounced along the dirt roads in Newberg, Bert stayed up the entire night boning up on physiology. As he reported the next day, "I triumphantly passed."

Bert thrilled to the words of the university's first president, Dr. David Starr Jordan, as he delivered the opening speech that memorable October day. "Our university has no history to fall back on. It is hallowed by no traditions. It is hampered by none. Its fingers all point forward."

But Bert was disappointed to learn that Dr. John Branner, head of the department of geology and mining, wouldn't be on campus until January. When Branner finally did arrive, Bert was happy to learn that with only 11 people in the geology class, Branner was able to give each student a great deal of personal attention. Bert was still painfully shy, and it took Branner several weeks to realize that behind that timid exterior was a sharp intelligence. Also recognizing Bert's resourcefulness and reliability, Branner hired him as a part-time secretary.

A Student Entrepreneur

The $30 a month Dr. Branner paid Bert gave him spending money, but he needed to earn more in order to pay future tuition and other expenses. In addition to carrying a full course load and holding the job with Branner, Bert managed to get a contract to deliver the San Francisco morning paper on campus. Pushing himself to the limits, he also became the laundryman for Stanford students. He would pick up the dirty laundry from faculty houses and students on Monday morning and return it on Saturday. When he was an upperclassman, he lent both businesses to other students and collected a percentage of the earnings.

As though Bert didn't already have enough to do, he also tried out for the school baseball team. After all, he had to let loose somehow. He surprised himself by doing so well as a shortstop that he became a regular on the team. However, an injury to his finger, which stayed with him all his life, forced him to give up playing.

Undaunted, Bert became manager of the baseball team. He sold tickets, scheduled games, and cared for equipment. The shy, quiet engineering student was acquiring a reputation for being a go-getter who got things done without fuss. He didn't even balk at asking a visiting former President of the United States, Benjamin Harrison, to pay a quarter at the gate as everyone else did. Harrison cheerfully gave Bert a dollar bill and said he'd buy a ticket for the following week also. When he refused the 50 cents in change Bert handed him, Bert, embarrassed but determined, told Harrison that Stanford was not a charitable institution. Harrison insisted that Bert keep the change, but he wouldn't give in. Finally, Harrison ended the impasse by buying two more tickets.

OUT OF THE CLASSROOM, INTO THE FIELD

Because Branner needed some field work done in the Ozarks, he made Bert an offer for the summer following his freshman year. The work would give Bert some practical experience, a modest salary, and a few hours of university credit. Bert jumped at the chance and spent July and August roaming the Ozark countryside, surveying instruments on his shoulder and a hammer in the belt of his overalls. He found the mountain people "hospitable but suspicious of all government agents. Some were moonshiners and to them even a gawky boy could be a spy."

The summer in the Ozarks influenced Bert for the rest of his life. He was shocked by the poverty and the poor diet, and was sure that generations spent eating only sowbelly, sorghum molasses, and cornmeal had "fatally lowered [the local people's] vitality and ambitions." His time in the Ozarks and his earlier boyhood summer with the impoverished Osage Indians fueled what was to be a lifetime commitment to feed the hungry of the world.

Bert loved his solitary, free life roaming the mountains and conducting his studies. He returned to Stanford "lean as a greyhound, as hard as nails," with nearly $200 to help pay for his sophomore year.

A classmate during Bert's sophomore year described him as being "very immature in appearance, probably the youngest looking of us all. He seemed shy to the point of timidity— rarely spoke unless spoken to. It wasn't until later, when we got into politics on the same side and I began to see under his surface, that I realized how much it was possible to like him."

Dr. Branner introduced Bert to another eminent geologist, Swedish-born Waldemar Lindgren, who was with the United States Geologic Survey. Hoover spent his second college summer with Dr. Lindgren covering miles on horseback in the "glorious High Sierra," and the deserts of Nevada. He tested rock samples, made careful notes, and turned out to be the best assistant Lindgren had ever had.

First Step in Politics

But Bert had more than geology on his mind that summer with Lindgren. Before he had left Stanford, a scandal had erupted over the sale of tickets to a university event. Bothered by this, Bert investigated the circumstances leading to the scandal and discovered that most of the college concerts, dances, and sporting events were run by students who were pocketing some of the ticket money. It was clear to Bert that the

Hoover (standing, 2nd from left) with instructors and fellow engineering students when he was a sophomore at Stanford University. (Herbert Hoover Presidential Library.)

university needed a new constitution that required all student activities to be handled by the student government. An elected and salaried treasurer would supervise all student events and keep audited records of money transactions.

Bert's supporters wanted him to run for treasurer, but he only consented to do so when they agreed that he would receive no salary. He did not want anyone to think that he had created a paying job for himself. It was a hard-fought campaign with all the political trappings: high-blown speeches, rallies, walls plastered with posters, even free cigars. Bert and his supporters won. The university had a new constitution, and the student government had its first treasurer.

A GOOD IDEA GOES BAD

Grandmother Minthorn died during Bert's sophomore year, and Tad had to leave college and work in a printer's office to support himself and May. Bert's determination that Tad return to college drove him to try to earn more money the next summer, but no work in the field materialized. The East Coast was suffering a financial collapse that was just beginning to cause hardship on the West Coast. Banks were closing, people were out of work, and there were hunger marches and strikes every day.

Bert puzzled over the causes of the "Panic of 1893." His mind, geared for efficiency, wanted to understand what had gone wrong. He made a promise to himself—when he completed his engineering courses, he would do some studying of economics on his own. In his scheme of things, everything had a cause and effect.

Since there was no money to be made doing work in geology, Bert and a few friends went to San Francisco with a plan in mind. He and his "company" would erect small bill-

boards along roads in the Yosemite Valley advertising products for any businessman smart enough to hire them. After
a newspaper and several companies signed contracts for work,
the sign-painting business was launched. Bert's group bought
a team of horses, camping equipment, paint, and signboards,
and with seemingly no concern for the eyesores they were
introducing into that magnificent country, they went about
fulfilling their contracts. Luckily, they went broke quickly,
having charged too little for their services.

A Long Hike to a New Job

The timing was perfect. Just at the moment of financial collapse of the sign-painting venture, Dr. Lindgren sent Bert a
telegram inviting him to join his geologic survey of the
Pyramid Peak quadrangle close to Lake Tahoe on the Cali-
fornia-Nevada border. Bert had no money to pay for stage-
coach fare to the railroad junction where the Lindgren group
would meet him. No matter. He said good-bye to his bank-
rupt friends and began hiking north over the mountains. He
walked 80 miles in three days and met Lindgren and his group
as promptly as if he had pulled up in a cab he had hailed
two miles away.

Bert and the "Barbs"

On campus Bert had become allied with the "Barbs"– short
for Barbarians, the name given by the elitist Greek fraternity men to those who did not belong to a fraternity. Though
only a minority of the student population, the "Greeks" controlled campus affairs because they had no organized opposition. Then a "Barb" by the name of Zion decided to run
for president of the student government.

Those students who were too poor to pay $23 a month

to live in Encina Hall lived in the "camp," a group of shacks behind the engineering building that once housed the laborers who built the university. They slept in bunks and cooked on kerosene stoves. Zion enlisted Bert's aid in bringing out the vote of the students in the "Camp."

Bert identified with the poor students and was able to win their trust. As he recalled in his memoirs, his first political conviction was that a university had to be run as a democracy. With Ray Lyman Wilbur, who became his closest friend at Stanford (and who was to become president of Stanford 50 years later), Bert delivered the "Camp's" vote, and Zion won by a small margin.

A NEW INTEREST

It was no wonder that Bert—busy with his studies, his various campus jobs, and as treasurer of the student government—would have little time for girls. It wasn't as if this tall, awkward, young man who often had trouble getting his words out in the right order would attract the typical Stanford coed anyhow.

"Typical" would never be the word used to describe Lou Henry. Brought up by a father who was a great outdoorsman and who saw no reason why girls shouldn't ride horses, hike in the mountains, or do rugged camping, she loved the wilderness and was well tutored in the ways of living with the sky as a roof. Lou was the first young woman from her hometown of Monterey, California, to go to college. Stanford, three years old by that time, had 800 students, 250 of them women. Most of the coeds were enrolled in the standard course for women—literature. But that was not where Lou's interests lay. Instead, she enrolled in the geology department, becoming its first woman student.

One morning, Lou and Dr. Branner were talking about a rock specimen when Bert walked in, fresh from a field trip in the High Sierras. He was a senior by that time but had lost little of his awkwardness. Dr. Branner asked Bert's opinion on the identification of the rock specimen, introducing him to Lou and telling him that she thought it was a specimen of the precarboniferous age.

Bert, taken completely off guard by this tall, lithe young woman with blue eyes and thick, shiny hair, managed to mumble a few words. His round face made him look a little boyish, despite his height and broad shoulders.

The next day Bert half ran to the geology laboratory. Would the blue-eyed girl with the easy smile be there? And what if she were? He slowed down. What would he say to her? Would his tongue get tied up in his mouth as it had the day before? Probably.

Bert didn't see Lou that day or the next. As senior in charge of Saturday geology expeditions for freshmen, Bert met with the students early the following Saturday morning. Lou came walking up in a hiking skirt and sturdy boots. From that Saturday on, Bert surprised Dr. Branner with his enthusiasm for leading the Saturday freshman expeditions.

Chapter 4

Three New Suits and a Beard

And what was there to attract Lou Henry to Bert Hoover? Did she see him as Will Irwin, a classmate of hers, did?

He was tall—just under six feet—broad shouldered, very lean figure. He wore one of those double-breasted blue suits which have since become almost a uniform with him. He had a slight stoop, you felt, came rather from excess muscular development of the shoulders than from the midnight oil. He carried his head a trifle to one side . . . and had mouse-colored hair, as stubbornly straight as an Indian's, and hazel eyes so contemplative they seemed dreamy. He often stood with one foot thrust forward, jingling the keys in his trouser pocket. . . . While he walked humanely among us, he was a kind of legend, a supernally able person.

MORE OR LESS ENGAGED

Lou didn't miss one of the Saturday geology hikes. At ease outdoors in a way he could never be in a classroom or living room, Bert was able, after a few weeks of hiking with Lou, to talk with her about subjects that had nothing to do with precarboniferous rocks. He learned that they had been born in Iowa in the same year and only 50 miles apart, and that they both had come to the West Coast when they were 10 years old. Lou's father was a banker, and though it was clear that Lou lived in luxury compared to Bert, she was down-to-earth, simple in her tastes, and used to pitching in and doing her share of work. As the only coed among the robust and adventuresome male engineering students, Lou fought the stereotype of a woman as being destined only for marriage, children, and the home.

Lou's power to enchant Bert was such that he even consented to let her teach him how to dance, something that he had never done, more from shyness than from any Quaker strictures against it. The tall, energetic pair became familiar as a couple on campus. Lou had tremendous respect for Bert's resourcefulness in managing to be financially independent, for his geologic know-how in the laboratory and in the field, for his integrity, and for his driving ambition, which made him eager for challenge and adventure. It became clear to all who knew Bert that from the time he met Lou Henry in the geology laboratory, no other girl existed for him.

When Bert was ready to graduate in 1895, Lou still had three more years of Stanford ahead of her. On graduation night, with the band playing "Auld Lang Syne," Bert could only manage to ask Lou to write to him. She understood him well enough to know that he felt he could ask no more of her than that. He had no job and no money. But by the time they said good-bye, they had an understanding that they were "more or less engaged."

STARTING FROM THE BOTTOM

During Stanford's early years, no grades were given: students passed, "conditioned," or flunked. Bert flunked one class during his whole four years—German. Dr. Branner, who believed in grounding his young engineering students in mathematics, geology, chemistry, physics, and civil engineering so they could shift to any branch of engineering they wanted, felt that Hoover's strong point was his originality. He attacked all problems in his own way and never stopped working until he obtained results.

It was a big disappointment for Hoover when, with his high expectations and his hard-earned diploma, he could not find a job in his chosen field. He tried to get on the staff of a gold mine in Nevada City, California but ironically, his college training worked against him. The head of the mine was an old prospector who regarded "college-bred" men as impractical and soft.

Hoover had to eat. He took a laborer's job with a shift of Cornish miners and pounded a drill, shoveled ore, and pushed a handcar for eight hours, day or night, in a mine whimsically called the "Mayflower." A Stanford classmate, E.B. Kimball, who was also working in the mines while waiting for a job to break, lived in the same boardinghouse as Hoover did. The two men spent their free time together loafing about the Nevada City Hotel, talking to miners and picking up the lore of the trade.

Moving Up

After earning enough money to buy a ticket to San Francisco, Hoover packed his bags and headed for the offices of Louis Janin. A highly respected mining engineer who had been educated in Paris and Freiberg, Germany, Janin was now working out of San Francisco. Sensing that Hoover was no ordinary engineer, Janin hired him. After a short time Janin was impressed enough to send Hoover off on engineering missions to mines in California, Nevada, New Mexico, and Arizona. Bert looked over new properties or studied the possibilities of developing old mines. He was building on the foundation that Branner and Lindgren had helped him lay, combining a broad knowledge of practical engineering with industrial management.

Bert always kept in close touch with Tad and May. When they moved to Berkeley, California—just across the bay from San Francisco—where May was going to college and Tad was working as a typesetter, Hoover would stay with them on his time off from the field. Always the planner, Hoover suggested that Tad go to an engineering school so the two of them could work in partnership some day. Hoover's confidence that this was the thing to do sold Tad. He enrolled in Stanford the next semester.

A New Assignment

What the two brothers did not know at that time was that Bert would be spending very little time in the United States during the next 10 years. A boom had hit Western Australia, where gold had been found in the Coolgardie district. Bewick, Moreing and Company, a British mining company with worldwide interests, hired Janin to send an expert engineer to Coolgardie who could introduce the Australians to the modern gold-mining technology developed in California. Janin, in an act of personal kindness—it was a sacrifice to give up the assistance of such a gifted young man—offered the job to Hoover.

"You'll need clothes," exclaimed two of his friends as Hoover tore home and told them the news. He was euphoric enough to let them lead him to a custom tailor's shop—he would be earning a dazzling $7,500 a year plus expenses. With his friends coaxing him on, he chose three suits. Then one of his friends who loved Scotch tweeds but couldn't afford them urged Bert into buying a "morning coat" of a rather loud tweed. Two years later the friend received a package from Hoover sent from Australia. It contained the coat and a note saying, "Since you like this . . . thing, take it. I haven't worn it yet."

Aging Quickly

Bewick, Moreing had requested that Janin send them a qualified man about 35 years of age to take over the Australian project. Hoover was not quite 24. His directions were to meet the company officers in London first, and then travel to Australia. In the little time he had before leaving San Francisco, Hoover stopped shaving and practically wished a beard into existence. On his farewell evening with his friends, the consensus was that the beard easily made him look all of 26 years old.

The elegant offices of Bewick and Moreing, Mr. Moreing's palatial home, where Hoover stayed for a weekend, along with the horrendous fact that a butler, Buttons, was assigned to him and insisted on helping him dress, made Hoover count the minutes before he could escape London for the wilds of Australia.

THE LAND "DOWN UNDER"

Hoover suffered from occasional bouts of nausea on the long, sometimes tedious, often fascinating, ocean voyage to Australia. So much of the world to see at one time! He hung over the rail, taking in everything, as the ship passed through the Bay of Biscay, sailed into the blue Mediterranean, and traveled along the coast of Africa to the island of Malta. The building of the Suez Canal was a great engineering achievement, and Hoover was excited by his passage through it, though it took almost two days and a night.

The seasons are reversed in the Southern Hemisphere, and Hoover arrived in Australia in mid-summer. He journeyed from fertile land fed by plentiful rainfall to the bleak desert of Coolgardie, where the only greenery was an occasional bleached sagebrush and the only animal life a lizard or dwarf kangaroo. A settlement of corrugated iron shacks

Hoover with gold prospectors on his first assignment in the remote back country of Australia. He was to travel around the world several times as a top international mining consultant. (Herbert Hoover Presidential Library.)

and bedraggled tents baked under a sun that kept the normal midnight temperature over 100 degrees.

"All that Glitters . . ."

Hoover quickly determined that the gold at Coolgardie was all on the surface—there were no deep veins to yield the coveted metal. Bewick and Moreing had land about 25 miles away in Kalgoorlie. Hoover shaved off his beard, wired the company that he was off to investigate possibilities in Kalgoorlie, and left on a buggy ride that took him through clouds of swirling dust across land so barren that a bit of sagebrush was an event.

Like Coolgardie, Kalgoorlie was made up of tents, iron shacks, and a population of grimy prospectors who never wasted precious water on bathing and shaving. The annual rainfall was only one inch! When it did rain, bells clanged and everyone dropped what they were doing to set out pans to catch the precious liquid.

But here there was gold, lots of it! Hoover watched prospectors as they scooped up a pan full of surface dust, then blew until the dust was gone and only gold specks remained. He created efficient procedures for the mine operators to lay out mines, plan development, and order new equipment. At first the operators were put off by Hoover's youthfulness, but they quickly realized that they had a true professional working with them and gave him the name "Chief," which stuck with Hoover for the rest of his life.

Hoover took on the challenge of devising a way to extract the gold from the ore and refine it on location. The lack of water and fuel had made this an unachievable goal until then. But the resourcefulness that Dr. Branner had felt was Hoover's strong point showed itself when Hoover reasoned that the desert bush, growing to a height of 10 feet, could be burned for fuel. And there actually was some undrinkable water available, pumped from shallow wells. With his staff, Hoover set about finding a way to obtain enough water for the gold separation and extraction process. Eventually they succeeded by developing a filter that enabled them to recycle the water. The filter was so successful that it became a standard tool in mine operations.

"The Sons of Gwalia"

Always on the search for new mines, Hoover assembled a camel caravan to take him and his staff 150 miles across the desert to an area called "The Sons of Gwalia." Hoover's uncanny sense of where gold was located told him that there was a real find here, and he cabled his recommendation to Bewick, Moreing that they buy a substantial portion of the property. The company cabled back that they had made the purchase he recommended and were appointing him manager of the Sons of Gwalia mine at $10,000 a year and expenses, plus a small percentage of the gold they mined.

Hoover was in his glory. He constructed a big corrugated iron residence hall, brought staff in (including some Stanford colleagues), and created a tiny compound next to Mt. Leonora, the highest mountain peak in Western Australia, rising all of 160 feet. To enliven the evenings for the staff, he had an entire library shipped from California and initiated an adult reading and discussion program.

Over the years, the Gwalia mines produced more than $55,000,000 in gold. In his memoirs, Hoover writes as if he singlehandedly developed the filter and the Sons of Gwalia mines. In both of these efforts he had the help of others which he did not acknowledge. This tendency to exaggerate his own accomplishments while failing to mention the efforts of others was puzzling for a man whose achievements in the field of engineering won him international fame, but it persisted to the end of his life.

New Horizons

In the summer of 1898, Bewick, Moreing made Hoover an offer that sent his head spinning: Go to China and direct all the mines owned by the Chinese Empire.

Lou Henry's mailbox yielded a letter from Bert that turned her life in a whole new direction. He was going to China on a big job, he wrote. Would she marry him so they could go on a Chinese honeymoon?

Lou's letter in return contained the one word Hoover wanted to read. Yes!

Chapter 5

Assignment in China

Bert Hoover and Lou Henry were married at high noon on Friday, February 10, 1899, in Monterey. The sun shone past the bright bougainvillea into the sitting room of the Henry house where a small number of wedding guests, including Tad and May, had gathered.

Both Lou and Bert were dressed in brown suits appropriate for travel. Lou's practical outfit was softened with a white lace blouse, but Bert's high white collar just increased the seriousness of his manner. The young couple joined hands in Quaker fashion and repeated their vows in a short civil ceremony. They left the flower-filled house at two o'clock to take the train to San Francisco, where they would depart by ship for China the next day.

ARRIVAL IN TIENTSIN

During their 3½-week trip across the Pacific, Lou and Bert holed up in their cabin and pored over the many books on Chinese culture that they had brought. It was March when the ship docked at the mouth of the Pei-ho River on the outskirts of Tientsin, the most important commercial city in

Hoover and Lou Henry (holding hat), with Charles, Jean, and Florence Henry (left to right), on their wedding day in Monterey, California. The next day they left for a honeymoon in China. (Herbert Hoover Presidential Library.)

northern China. Ricksha boys pulling squeaking one-passenger, two wheeled carts dashed in and out of traffic, narrowly avoiding collisions. Lou averted her eyes from the sight of the coolies (laborers who work for low wages) pulling carts so heavy that the ropes rubbed sores on their bare shoulders. Nothing she had read in the seclusion of their shipboard cabin prepared her for the change from her sheltered life in quiet Monterey to this teeming, raw city, ruled by Kwang Hsu, the "Boy Emperor."

Envy and Suspicion

Bert and Lou moved into an attractive blue brick house in the foreign settlement of Tientsin. However, they weren't given a particularly cordial welcome by their neighbors. Hoover's rapid rise in his field and the executive power he wielded made some of his peers envious of him. Then there were those who were suspicious of the new couple's eagerness to immerse themselves in Chinese life, especially when, imbued with the Quaker belief in democracy, the Hoovers ignored the local caste system (division of society into social classes) and made friends with Chinese of all ranks.

Bert and Lou liked to walk through the lantern-lit city at night, the evening air pungent with the aroma of incense burning in the many small shops that opened out on the narrow streets. They threaded their way through the crush of sedan chairs and rickshas to look at the fine silks, carved jewels, and embroidered clothing on display. Lou fell in love with the porcelain and bought the first of many exquisite pieces that would someday become one of the world's finest porcelain collections. Hoover's collecting took a different turn. He began accumulating books on China that he eventually gave to Stanford to form the nucleus of its Chinese Library.

"Find Gold"

Hoover's chief responsibility for the Chinese Mining and Engineering Company was to build an ice-free, coal-loading port on the Gulf of Chihli, about 150 miles northeast of Tientsin. It was a task that he managed to do with impressive ease. Another responsibility was tied up with the complicated politics of China. The Empress Dowager, a brilliant, shrewd, and selfish woman, had ruled China for decades when her son, the Boy Emperor, took over and instituted a "Reform and Progress Movement" to modernize China.

Kwang Hsu, the Boy Emperor, appointed Chang Yen-Mao to head the government's Bureau of Mines. The Empress Dowager however, became unhappy with her position as second in command. She arranged to have her son imprisoned and took over leadership of the country again. Chang then felt that he had to prove his worth to the Empress Dowager, and he decided the way to do it was to "find gold . . . much gold."

That was the directive Chang gave to young Hoover. But Bert tried to convince Chang that it would be of much greater benefit to China if he found coal, iron, lead, zinc, and copper deposits. Chang, however, wanted gold, and set up a trip for Hoover to the reputedly rich Jebol Province. Hoover's caravan consisted of 100 cavalry officers, a general, government officials, a cook, grooms, 10 extra ponies, 100 mules, and a long line of carts.

However, hundreds of gold-hungry prospectors had already scratched the earth of Jebol for its scant treasure. Chang was not happy to hear Hoover's cheerless report, in which he said that over dozens of centuries the Chinese had "mined every shred of metal down to water level." But Chang would not give up. He sent Hoover out to check other possible mines that he had heard about. Hoover found no gold, but he did discover an anthracite coal field west of Peking that eventually yielded more coal than all other coal deposits combined elsewhere in the world.

The Man with the Green Eyes

Wherever he went in China, news of Hoover's coming usually preceded him. Villagers would gather in the road to stare at him as he entered their settlement. They believed that his green eyes gave him the power to see into the earth and find gold. Never had they seen green eyes before!

Hoover's explorations took him into Manchuria, Mongolia, and into the Chihli, Shantung, and Shansi provinces. His pack-mules carried a good supply of books by Balzac, Rousseau, Zola, and Hugo to help him fight boredom and loneliness in his nightly encampments, where bedbugs and filth were routine. Though Lou wanted to join him, Bert felt that many of these places were too primitive and unsanitary for her.

THE BOXER REBELLION

By 1900 anti-foreign demonstrations were becoming more and more frightening as a wave of hatred for Caucasians (white people) was washing over China. In 1889 the Boy Emperor had brought in foreign experts to help realize his dream of modernizing China. When the Empress Dowager dethroned her son, she created the impression that all of China's hardships were caused by the foreigners invited in by the Boy Emperor. Secret societies calling themselves "The Plum Blossom Fists," "The Mailed Fist," and "The Fist of Public Harmony" were formed to fight the intrusion of these "foreign devils." (The foreigners mistakenly thought that these groups were prize-fighting clubs and called them "the Boxers.") The Empress Dowager fueled the fanaticism of these extremists, who slaughtered 250 missionaries in northeastern China and 30,000 Chinese they had converted to Christianity.

Attack on Tientsin

Lou and Bert, in their home in Tientsin, learned that the Boxers had targeted Peking and Tientsin for their next assault. On June 10, 1900, shells bursting in the air woke them from their sleep and catapulted them into a nightmare that lasted a full month.

Because their house was situated on a hill, it was an obvious target. So the Hoovers moved into the home of their friends, the Drews, which was protected by a high wall. Others in the foreign settlement joined them, and the Drew house became a dormitory; women slept on the floor in one room, men in another. One side of the settlement was protected by a river. On the unprotected sides, Hoover directed the building of a barricade across the exposed open fields and spaces between the houses. The protective wall was several feet high and consisted of sugar barrels, sacks of peanuts, and bags of grain.

When news came that the Chinese Army had joined the Boxers, Hoover was consumed with worry over Lou ever getting out of China alive. But Lou was undaunted, insisting that she did not want to be anywhere else but with her husband. After sweeping spent bullets off the lawn, she would get on her bicycle, pedal to the compound hospital, and nurse the hundreds of wounded brought in each day. When a bullet punctured the front wheel of her bike, she walked.

Relief at Last

After three weeks, the Hoovers heard, to their intense relief, that American and Japanese soldiers were coming to fight the Boxers from the Philippines, British from Shanghai, and French from Indo-China. Four American war correspondents, among them the flamboyant California poet Joaquin Miller, were part of the first American contingent to reach Tientsin. Miller decided that he was going to see Peking as long as he was in China. Lou, Bert, and everyone else told him he was walking into a deathtrap, but he ignored their warnings and arranged for a ricksha to take him to Peking. But a short time after he started out on his mad journey, the ricksha boy he had hired deserted him, and Miller returned to the compound furious and frustrated. Lou didn't tell Miller that she had secretly bribed the ricksha boy to abandon him en route.

On July 15 a Chinese boy brought the message that United States Marines had been sighted. Hoover climbed to the top of the highest building in the Tientsin settlement and saw the Marines approaching. Their bugle corps was playing "There'll be a Hot Time in the Old Town Tonight." Never had the music sounded so beautiful!

The Marine colonel decided to lead an assault against the enemy in their own fortresses and asked Hoover to be his guide. Hoover agreed, despite his Quaker beliefs. When Marines next to him were shot, he even asked for a gun, but he never fired it. The Boxer forces finally collapsed, and the Empress Dowager fled with her entourage to the interior of China.

With the Empress Dowager went the Bureau of Mines and Hoover's job. He and Lou decided it was time to return home to California. Tientsin, which had been so alive with people, speeding rickshas, merchant's voices, and temple music when they had arrived a year and a half before, was now a place of death and ruin. Three-quarters of its houses were rubble. The screaming of falling shells was still in Lou and Bert's ears as they made their way through the mourners to board the tugboat that took them down the Pei-ho River. There they boarded the steamer that would carry them on the first lap of their journey home.

Chapter 6

"Chief"

L ou and Bert were not to return to California to stay after all. Bewick, Moreing offered Hoover a junior partnership and the chance to travel to their mines throughout the world. They wanted to use his expertise in mining to make their operations more effective. There would be time, too, to explore any new sites his uncanny green eyes could ferret out.

It was 1901, the dawn of the 20th century. The automobile, railroad, plumbing, electrical, highway-building, and telephone industries were growing with stunning speed. All the new constructions, technology, and products gobbled up the raw materials buried in the earth. As one historian reported, it was the golden age for the mining engineer who "scoured the earth and tapped the soil to meet the hungry needs of industrial development."

THE WORLD'S FINEST

It was a perfect time for Hoover to build his career. Within the next 13 years, he was to circle the globe numerous times, discovering and developing mines in Burma, Ethiopia, South Africa, Egypt, and Russia. Tailors on four continents had his measurements so that he could get on the phone and order a suit for a suddenly convened meeting no matter where he was.

In all of his endeavors, Hoover was mindful of the basic Quaker tenet to "create a social and economic system which will so function as to sustain and enrich life for all." He paid the highest wages of any of the gold fields in the world and was always concerned about the working conditions of his miners, although he was accused by competitors of callousness and profiteering. He was given the coveted gold medal by the Society of Mining and Metallurgical Engineers, made president of the society, and generally recognized as the world's finest mining engineer. By the year 1913, he could count over 175,000 men working for him in his far-flung enterprises.

Hoover operated on a high energy level to the point of exhaustion. Restless, probing, hard to satisfy, still the introvert, he had a hard time slowing down to take a vacation. When he did, he buzzed through the sights so quickly it was as if he had an internal clock ticking away reminding him of hours that could be spent more productively.

When Lou managed to get him to go on a picnic with friends, Bert would soon be knee deep in mud, damming streams, constructing canals, and building sluices. He would invite anyone who came by to join him in the mud and help gather stones for his miniature engineering projects.

A Man on the Go

Lou had an exile's hunger to return to her native country, establish a permanent home, and begin a family. But as was to be the pattern throughout her life, she put her husband's needs before her own; she agreed that Bewick, Moreing's offer of a junior partnership was too good to pass up. Yet she was a strong-willed woman with her own opinions and high standards. Once a course of action was agreed upon, she participated fully with Hoover in carrying it out.

So London was to be their home base, not California, and Bert and Lou furnished a comfortable apartment for themselves in Hyde Park Gate. But to give them the "back home" connection they so sorely craved, they built a cottage in Monterey while in California for the summer of 1902. Hoover, though exhilarated by his globe-trotting experiences, harbored a real longing for a home in his own country. Although he was able to get along fine with the rulers of China and the villagers of Kalgoorlie, he always felt himself an alien, sometimes even a trespasser. No one would know this, of course, except Lou. To the world, he was a "man on the go," with fame, fortune, and a devoted, intelligent wife.

HOME SWEET MOVEABLE HOME

Hoover's first assignment as a junior partner in Bewick, Moreing was to inspect the company's mines in Australia. Lou wanted to go with him and he agreed. He was excited about showing her places he had talked about for so long. That pleasure chilled a little when he learned they were to live deep in the interior country in Kalgoorlie, still inhabited by aborigines (local natives) and plagued by the crushing heat he remembered all too well. But Lou, with her usual flare, converted a nondescript Bewick, Moreing company house into a cheerful and interesting home filled with the artifacts that she and Bert loved to collect.

The year and a half they spent in Australia and then in Burma passed quickly. After Hoover completed his work, he and Lou returned to London, where Bert promised that they would buy a house and "settle down." It was time. Lou was pregnant, and they were both excited over the prospect of being parents. On Christmas eve of 1902, they spent a happy time with the general manager of Bewick, Moreing at his home, enjoying the fun of Christmas with his four children. Soon they would have their own child to wake up on Christmas morning.

A Near Disaster

The news Bert called to tell Lou a few days later was almost impossible to believe. The general manager of Bewick, Moreing had disappeared, leaving a 20-page letter confessing that he had borrowed over $700,000 on the security of the firm and had forged its name to papers. Hoover felt that the company was morally responsible for the money and had to pay its creditors every single penny. Bewick was in Canada hunting moose; Moreing was in Manchuria. He cabled them, and they replied that the company was not responsible for the losses.

Hoover, however, felt he had no other option but to pay the company's debts out of his own pocket. In one day, he and Lou saw their life's savings nearly demolished, but Bert remained calm in the face of this personal disaster. Because Bewick and Moreing eventually did pay back 75 percent of the loss, and another junior partner paid back the other 25 percent, the setback for Bert and Lou was only momentary. The general manager was later arrested and jailed, and for years the Hoovers faithfully sent a monthly allowance to the manager's destitute mother, whom they had met only once in their lives.

A FAMILY OF GLOBE-TROTTERS

While Hoover was traveling during Lou's pregnancy, she remained in London preparing equipment so that mother and child could accompany Bert on an expected trip to Australia. Herbert Clark Hoover, Jr., was born on August 4, 1903. Five weeks later he was traveling in a blanket-lined basket to Australia. The sturdy little boy traveled around the world with his mother and father two times by the time he was a year old.

When Hoover had to leave his family behind, he kept in touch by mail. Lou was a good researcher, and he would often ask her to look up some information in the Library of the British Museum. During one of her research assignments, Lou stumbled upon an old copy of Georgius Agricola's *De re Metallica.* The book, originally published in Latin in 1556, had once been the standard manual of mining and metallurgy. Intrigued by the publication, Lou and Bert embarked on the time-consuming, engrossing project of translating it.

The years that Lou and Bert had spent studying Latin at Stanford paid off. While Hoover was traveling, Lou kept working on the translation. They accumulated over 2,500 rare books on the subject of medieval mining during the course of the five years it took to complete the project.

An enlightened man beyond his times, Agricola had put forth in his book a case for reformed labor practices—the eight-hour day, different kinds of insurance, and the creation of guilds for the exchange of knowledge. In his notes to the translation, Hoover strongly supported the eight-hour day and the establishment of labor unions. He dedicated the book to his old professor, John Branner, and was as proud of it as he was of any of the many mines he developed.

An Ambitious Project

In the summer of 1905, Hoover went to the tiny country of Burma, in Southeast Asia, to see whether the legends that spoke of rich silver mines in the area were true. For centuries man had known how to obtain silver by refining lead ore and had told tales of the fantastic silver mines in the Burma area that created fabulous wealth for the Ming Dynasty of China during the 14th and 15th centuries.

Hoover confirmed that there were indeed rich minerals to be mined in Burma, but it would require a great deal of money to build roads through the jungle and to cross mountains with a railroad and bridges. He rushed back to London to make the necessary financial arrangements and had so much faith in the project that he invested much of his own savings in it.

It took several years to complete the railroad, giving thousands of Burmese much-needed work. Under the guidance of Hoover and his staff, bridges were built and a smelting plant constructed. Benefiting the economy of Burma and Hoover's growing fortune, the rich ore rolled out of the jungles in railroad cars to Mandalay, the site of the smelting plant, and the minerals then traveled to international markets.

"A Happy Shop"

By 1908 the mines in Burma had prospered enough for Hoover to leave his partnership with Bewick, Moreing. With Henry Clark Hoover, Jr., now age five, and Allan, age one, Bert and Lou moved to California, where he opened his own engineering firm with offices in San Francisco, New York, London, Paris, and St. Petersburg (now Leningrad). His brother Tad, a practicing engineer, joined Bert's staff, as did many other young and talented men. It was "a happy shop," Hoover said, involved in the "sheer joy of creating productive enterprises."

Getting Involved

Despite frequent trips to his overseas offices, Hoover was now in the United States enough to become involved in campaigning for the presidential election of 1912. He was an enthusiastic supporter of Teddy Roosevelt, believing that big business needed some dramatic reforms. He was disappointed when Roosevelt lost to Woodrow Wilson and was determined to be even more active in the next presidential campaign.

Bert, Lou, and their two sons regularly spent their summers in London, in a home they called Red House, near Kensington Gardens. In the Quaker tradition, Hoover extended his hospitality to strangers as well as friends. He liked having company at dinner and yet he could go through a whole meal without uttering a word. His nephews and nieces devised a secret game. Who could make Uncle Bert talk first?

Back home in California, a visitor might find Hoover relaxing with his sons by panning for gold in the fountain in their yard. Bert, like the rest of America, had no preparation for what the imminent assassination of the Archduke Ferdinand, heir to the throne of Austria-Hungary, was about to do to their well-ordered lives.

Chapter 7

"The Slippery Road of Public Life"

Hoover was appalled at the thought of war. In his engineering work, which took him to countries all over the world, he had seen bitter tensions and economic disarray which made that bloody prospect only too real. He had observed the disturbing build-up of the German military machine, and the concern among the French and Russians, who, in self-defense, began to expand their own military arsenals.

Returning home late at night from his London office, Hoover would confide only a small part of his worries to Lou. But she knew he was keeping in close touch with his international business interests in case quick action was needed. If war erupted, his substantial holdings might be lost. That threat became painfully real when, less than a month after the assassination of Archduke Ferdinand in Sarajevo, Austria-Hungary served an ultimatum on Serbia.

WAR IN EUROPE

The stock market grew shaky as Europe responded by mobilizing its armies. On July 25, 1914, the British stock market crashed, and Hoover immediately cabled to his mines worldwide to cut down production. Three days later, Austria-Hungary declared war on Serbia. Fearing that the banks might close, which they did, Hoover withdrew enough money to meet his payroll. Bad news came with the morning coffee. Germany declared war on Russia, then on France.

From his office window, Hoover could see British troops marching. The sound of their boots hitting the pavement was ominous. He prayed that England would not enter the war.

Helping Stranded Americans

In an urgent phone call, the American consul in London, Robert P. Skinner, informed Hoover that the consulate office was swamped with frantic Americans who were rendered penniless when the banks closed. He appealed to Hoover to help him get cash to these people so that they could return home.

Hoover did not want to take on the job, but in all good conscience, he could not refuse Skinner. He hurried to the consulate's office, ordered the people to line up, and doled out the few hundred dollars he had in his own pocket. He then started on the task of finding housing for these people while he secured more financial aid.

Hoover had plans to leave with Lou and his sons for California at the end of the summer, but his ship was rerouted to Germany. No matter. He would not have left in any case. Unable to refuse both the U.S. consul and the ambassador, who begged him to direct the American Relief Committee, Hoover took on one of the most challenging and frustrating tasks of his career—that of engineering the return home of thousands of stranded Americans. He did not realize then that he was leaving engineering forever to enter on what he later called the "slippery road of public life."

Working out of the elegant ballroom at the Savoy Hotel,

Hoover directed the emergency rescue operation. He managed to get 500 volunteers to help him, many of whom had worked for him before and welcomed a chance to be on his team again. The reputation he had built as a businessman of integrity and as an organizational genius helped him secure the money he needed from American and British corporations. Within six weeks and with the help of Lou as well as his volunteers, he obtained food, clothing, and transatlantic passage for 120,000 anxious Americans.

The Missing Trousseau

The gargantuan job was relieved occasionally by some light moments. When a wealthy American socialite complained about losing her $5,000 trousseau, Hoover, playing detective, learned that it had found its way into the Old Clothes Department of the relief operation. There, the trousseau had been doled out, dress by dress, to destitute women who had never dreamed of being clothed in such finery. And when a dowager demanded a written guarantee that German submarines would not sink the ship she was on while returning to the United States, Hoover, without a blink of the eye, wrote one out for her.

When the dreaded finally happened—England declared war against Germany—there was the added emergency of getting American students who were attending overseas schools back home safely. Lou organized a women's committee to care for any unattended students, and Hoover and his able helpers secured American and other neutral ships to transport them to the United States. The success of their rescue operation proved to Hoover the effectiveness of voluntary service, which to him was the uniquely American way of getting a societal need fulfilled.

Relief for Belgium

Hoover had no sooner closed up shop in the Savoy ballroom when he was asked to head the Belgian relief program. Germany had occupied the whole of that tiny country in preparation for its assault on France. Belgium, relying for 80 percent of its food on imports, was facing starvation when the German invaders seized cattle and crops. The Allies then established a blockade to prevent any food that the Germans might snatch from coming in.

It was clear to Hoover that he could make millions of dollars by selling metals from his mines to those countries that were now arming themselves. But it was abhorrent to him to contribute to the killing of human beings, no matter who they might be. On the other hand, could he abandon his employees, his clients, and colleagues to take on this new relief mission? Could he afford to give up all of his income? His worldwide holdings were dangerously threatened by the shakiness of the international market. Yet he could not accept a salary. How could he appeal to others to work as volunteers when he was not doing so himself?

Will Irwin, a Stanford friend, was Hoover's house guest in London at this time of decision. Irwin, in his book on Hoover, described that fateful morning.

> Hoover bade me good morning, poured and sweetened his coffee, looked up, and—"Well, let the fortune go to hell," he said. In that phrase was born the Commission for Relief in Belgium (CRB). I felt then, I know now, that I had witnessed a significant moment in history.

FEEDING THE HUNGRY

That afternoon in October 1914 Hoover was on the phone ordering 10 million bushels of wheat from the Chicago commodity exchange. He, like most other Americans, believed that the war would be over by the following summer, and if he could manage to tide the Belgians over until the fall harvests, his task would have been completed. Never had he so miscalculated the length of a mission. He was on the job for 60 hours a week for four years! In that time he and his staff raised a billion dollars and transported five million tons of food to Belgium. He was constantly traveling to foreign capitals to argue, demand, exhort, and plea for support for a nation dying of starvation.

Hoover's toughest job of negotiation was with both the Germans and the British. The Germans were not providing the starving Belgian people with any food, claiming that they had to feed their own people first. They were also afraid of running out of supplies if they were to take on the feeding of an additional 10 million Belgians. The British were adamant that the German invaders were obligated to feed the occupied country. Furthermore, if the British were to feed the Belgians, this would help the German cause. As powerful a figure as Winston Churchill strongly opposed feeding the Belgians for this reason.

The Undiplomatic Diplomat

But Hoover would not give up. In a letter to Lloyd George, then Chancellor of the Exchequer, he communicated his sense of desperation. How could people of good conscience knowingly let their fellow man starve to death? By then, Hoover himself had pledged personal responsibility for sums of money that were far in excess of what he had.

"Except for the breadstuffs imported by this Commission, there is not one ounce of bread in Belgium today," Hoover wrote to Lloyd George, raising the specter of thousands upon thousands of dying men, women, and children.

"You have made a good fight, and deserve to win out," the Chancellor replied and sent Hoover money.

Winston Churchill, as well as many other high government officials, bridled at Hoover's aggressiveness, abruptness, sometimes impertinence in going all out for what the CRB needed. He could be the most "undiplomatic of diplomats," according to one official. He thought nothing of cabling the governor of Kansas that he "must" contribute several shiploads of wheat. Though the heads of state might wish he would disappear, grateful Belgians by the thousands put Hoover's picture up in their homes.

An Intrepid Wife

In the meantime, Lou Hoover had settled Herbert, Jr., and Allan in a boarding school in California, with relatives close by to care for them, and then rejoined Hoover in London. Hoover did not take for granted the sacrifice she made leaving her sons to work along side of him. He was to write that she "intrepidly [bravely] defied the dangers of the North Sea and went with me on my second trip to Brussels where we visited every sort of relief activity. . . . She was greatly affected by the spiritual tragedy which had overwhelmed the Belgian people. Her question was, 'Do these Germans think they can hold a people whose very souls revolt?' "

"Engineering" a New Cracker

Lou was particularly worried about the epidemics that were breaking out among the Belgian children. Hoover sought the aid of professional nutritionists from California and learned that the diet an adult might live on was insufficient for grow-

As director of the Commission for Relief in Belgium, Hoover instituted daily nutritional lunches in the public schools. (Herbert Hoover Presidential Library.)

ing children. He and his staff thereupon established a nourishing noonday meal in schools and other public institutions, at which time a cracker was served created by his nutritionists that contained every fat and vitamin a child needed. With the cracker went stew and condensed milk. Hoover liked to point out that his program was so successful that when the war ended, the mortality (death rate) of Belgian children was lower than ever before in that country's history.

Avoiding Publicity

Wary about attacks that could be made on someone handling such vast sums of money, Hoover had, upon assuming the job of directing the CRB, immediately hired an auditor to monitor the funds that went through his personal bank account. He was therefore prepared to open his books when a University of Michigan professor called the Belgian relief program "an elaborate system of graft." Incensed, Hoover notified the president of the university of the charges, which the professor subsequently dropped.

Ironically, Hoover, who was the first international figure to recognize and use the power of publicity, hated it when that publicity was focused on him. He opposed making public any list of charitable contributions lest "it be made the basis of expressions of gratitude with which we are already overwhelmed." He frustrated his assistants when he didn't show up to receive an important award in Brussels. Awards, he said, were "undemocratic."

To Quakers, good works become tainted if advertised. Hoover was pressed into accepting two decorations after the end of the war—The French Legion of Honor and that of Honorary Citizen and Friend to the Belgian Nation. Along with the latter award he was also given a Belgian passport with the stamp "Perpetual."

"It Pays to Advertise"

One of Hoover's main relief strategies was to see that the work of the CRB was widely advertised. He set up a tour for several American journalists to Belgium, his good friend Will Irwin among them. As one of the journalists later wrote, "The press campaign in America created a public opinion in the world that Germany and England always take into account, a public opinion that has not only saved Belgium from famine and worse, but from destruction and dismemberment as a nation. It pays to advertise!"

AMERICA AT WAR

But it was becoming increasingly more difficult for the United States to maintain its neutrality. At the beginning of the hostilities in Europe, President Wilson had offered the services of the United States as a mediator and had begun to write down his ideas for world peace by creating an association of nations. However, despite Wilson's efforts to remain neutral, Americans were turning more and more toward support for the Allies. Then, on May 7, 1915, the British passenger ship *Lusitania* was sunk without warning by a German submarine, killing nearly 1,200 persons, including 124 Americans. Anti-German sentiment in the United States became explosive. Although President Wilson wrote three different notes to the German government asking for reparations, he received no satisfactory reply.

Some months later, Wilson learned of a note sent by the German foreign secretary, Arthur Zimmermann, to the German ambassador in Mexico offering Mexico a piece of southwestern United States if it would join Germany and declare war on the United States.

Realizing that America could no longer remain neutral, Wilson summoned Hoover and asked if Belgian relief would be cut off if the United States entered the war. Hoover responded that Holland and Spain might take over the operation because they were both neutral.

On April 16, 1917, the United States declared war on Germany. Soon after, Wilson asked Hoover to return to Washington and take over as U.S. Food Administrator. Hoover agreed to serve as he had in the past, with no pay, believing that "the position will carry more moral leadership if I volunteer alongside of my countrymen."

With dread in his heart, Hoover closed up Red House and boarded a ship to cross the Atlantic on yet another trip home. It was a worried and sad homecoming, knowing that it was his own countrymen who would now be dying on the blood-soaked battlefields of Europe, far from the West Branches, the Montereys, and the Palo Altos they loved.

Chapter **8**

The Food King

On a balmy May day in 1917, Lou Hoover waited on the dock as the ocean liner pulled into New York harbor. Bert would be disembarking, but there was a difference in this homecoming that excited her. In the last three years, during his work with Belgian relief, Hoover had spent no more than six months with his sons. Now that he was Food Administrator and based in Washington, D.C., both she and Bert anticipated that they would be able to spend more family time together with Herbert, Jr., now 14, and Allan, now 10.

FOOD TO WIN THE WAR

The first item on Hoover's list of things to do with his sons was to plant a war garden in the backyard. He would do in his home what he would expect the American public to do. Food was needed to win the war. The country had to reduce food consumption and increase food production. "Remember, don't help the Hun at meal time," was one of the slogans plastered on billboards across the nation.

Hoover did not want to copy Europe and impose food rationing on citizens. He staunchly believed that if he could get the message across to Americans that winning the war depended on everyone's individual effort in food conservation, the country would respond.

Hoover had successfully opposed Wilson's plan to have the food program run by a commission of several equal members. The divided authority of commissions only lead to putting off decisions, he contended. A single official should be in charge of the program, a person who can control the operation from "the soil to the stomach." Working with volunteers would prevent him from deviating from democratic principles in which he believed so strongly.

Hoover, again taking no salary, recruited talented people. Among them were the sons of two former presidents, Dr. Harry Garfield and Robert Taft. Lewis Straus, who was 22 years old at the time and who would eventually become chairman of the Atomic Energy Commission, became Hoover's private secretary.

Hoover brought the hard facts to the American people — in 1916 and now in 1917 there was a severe crop failure. At the close of 1917 a British food official wrote Hoover that unless he was able to send the Allies "at least 75,000,000 bushels of wheat over and above what you have exported up to January first . . . I cannot take the responsibility of assuring our people that there will be enough food to win the war."

"Hooverizing"

By voluntary control of their food intake, Hoover said, Americans would be able to ensure that the needs of England, France, the American military machine, and the homefront could be met. His staff figured out what the dietary requirements of the average person were, and over 200,000 Americans signed pledges saying that they would live up to the Food Administration's guidelines. Buttons were passed out, as were membership cards that carried a Hoover-inspired message: "Go back to simple food, simple clothes, simple pleasures:

*As the country's Food Administrator during World War I,
Hoover called upon the American people to conserve food
voluntarily and help win the war. Posters like this one became
a part of the American scene.* (Library of Congress.)

Pray hard, work hard, sleep and play hard. Do it all courageously and cheerfully. We have a victory to win."

Though Lou hated public speaking, she made an appearance in New York to ask for support of the food conservation program. "There is some individual who is unknowingly dependent upon you for life: maybe a soldier in the trenches or a little child or peasant woman. They will not have anything to eat next spring if we don't think of them now."

Conserving food became a national endeavor and was given the name "hooverizing." Housewives observed wheatless and meatless days, and children sang songs about the delicious and nutritious "patriotic potato." The word "hooverizing" became so common a part of the American vocabulary that it even found its way into Valentine messages. "I can hooverize on dinner, and on lights and fuel too, but I'll never learn to hooverize when it comes to loving you."

The Driving Force

America did not disappoint Hoover. In a report to Wilson at the end of the first year of operations, Hoover was able to say that exports of wheat and other important food products were between 35 and 50 percent higher than the preceding year.

Hoover was called the "Food Czar" and the "Food Dictator" by those who found his style arrogant and alienating. He no doubt had a "short fuse," and was extremely impatient with people whom he thought lacked perception and intelligence. He was criticized for being devoid of compassion, "mechanical." When he was working fourteen-hour days and presenting statistics, issuing memos, directing strategies, relentlessly pursuing what he conceived of as his personal mission, Hoover gave little hint of his compassion for the world's hungry, which was the force that drove him on, day after day.

That compassion, however, seemed to be expressed only toward groups in general. Hoover avoided face-to-face encounters with people and was in misery when any contingent of the hungry he had helped came to thank him. Because of his distaste for personal publicity, the American people saw only that part of Hoover that was the efficient, impersonal engineer. They did not see the compassionate Hoover who wrote in his memoirs:

> It is impossible for someone who has never seen real famine to picture it — the pallid faces, the unsmiling eyes, the thin, anemic, bloated children, the dead pall over towns where children no longer play in the streets, the empty shops, the dumb, listless movements and dumb grief of women; the sweep of contagious diseases and the processions of funerals.

No Federal Control

In following what he believed to be the way to run a democratic society, Hoover avoided federal control and gave states and local municipalities the power to run their own food programs. Every state had its own food controller who worked with city and county volunteers. But the guiding ideas for the programs were originated by Hoover. As he explained before a Senate committee, "My idea is that we must centralize ideas but decentralize execution."

Hoover constantly pressed President Wilson to make just one man responsible for major undertakings instead of appointing commissions. On Hoover's recommendations, Wilson appointed federal administrators with the authority to run fuel, railroad, and shipping operations. These directors, along with the Cabinet secretaries of those government departments involved in the war effort, made up what Hoover called "The War Council." He was at the hub of the country's leadership and was among the closest advisors to President Wilson.

The boy is father to the man, as the old saying goes. The young student who Professor Branner praised for his resourcefulness and originality in getting things done was alive and well in the mature man who did not stop at using "abnormal methods for abnormal times." Seeing that unrestricted price competition in a world at war would hurt the living standard of low-income people, Hoover initiated price constraints on wheat, the most vital single food product. By setting up the United States Grain Corporation, which controlled all grain provisions for military and export purposes, Hoover managed to stabilize wheat prices.

Food for Germany

Despite all there was to do in the United States, Hoover never forgot the hungry women and children in Germany. Allied leaders thought his plan to lift the blockade long enough to enable German women and children to be fed was bizarre, even unpatriotic. As Hoover wrote in his memoirs:

> I do not believe in starving women and children. I do not believe it was the effective weapon of which the Allies were so confident. And above all, I did not believe that stunted bodies and deformed minds in the next generation were the foundation upon which to build civilization.

As one historian has suggested, had Hoover's approach been followed to a greater extent in World War I, the chances of a Hitler emerging in Germany would probably have been reduced. There would have been "fewer of those stunted bodies and deformed minds," susceptible of being led by a man of such monumentally antihuman policies.

THE WAR ENDS

During the fall of 1918, a virulent influenza epidemic that was engulfing the world hit Washington. Fortunately, the two Hoover sons were in California. More than half of the staff of the Food Administration became ill. Many of these workers were women volunteers far from home, and Lou organized nursing care for them in a girl's club dormitory. The epidemic spread quickly, killing 300,000 people in the United States and over 800,000 in Europe, more than had been killed in the war that year.

What joy then, in the midst of such sorrow, to hear the jubilant news that the Germans had asked President Wilson for an armistice. On November 11, 1918, the armistice was signed, bringing the fighting to an end.

A New Relief Mission

Now, Lou thought, they could begin living as a family again. But again she was wrong. Six days after the armistice, Lou and her two sons were at the boat dock in New York harbor bidding Hoover good-bye. He was bound for Europe, having been appointed by President Wilson to be director of the American Relief Administration. Again, Hoover had taken on another relief mission, putting aside his personal desires to spend time with his family and recoup some of his financial losses. There was no way, as he recounts in his memoirs, that he could, in good conscience, have refused:

> Ten million men were dead or maimed. Ten million men, women, and children had died of starvation and disease. Towns, cities, ships, railways were destroyed. . . . We knew from the Commission for Relief in Belgium experience that there were legions of starving waifs and subnormal children throughout Europe who must have special care at once if they

were not to become a generation of incompetents and criminals.

Hoover estimated that there were at least 150,000 children who needed food and care! No wonder then that for the next year he and his assistants, Will Irwin again among them, held meetings and had appointments straight through the day, including at mealtime. The directive he issued to his staff in the field was always the same: "Feed the hungry, only quickly!"

Peace Negotiations

Little more than a month after the armistice, on December 18, 1918, President Wilson arrived in Paris for the peace negotiations. He had drawn up a peace proposal, called the "Fourteen Points," months before and had presented it to Congress, advocating what he called "peace without victory." This meant a peace that would not exact revenge on Germany and Austria by demanding huge reparations. He also advocated a League of Nations, "an association of the nations, all bound together for the protection of the integrity of each."

Hoover, feeling that Wilson's ability to negotiate a strong peace would be jeopardized if he did not win Congress over to his policies, left the Republican ranks and supported the Democrats in the election of 1918, an act that many Republicans regarded as heresy. Americans were divided into two factions: those who supported Wilson and his League of Nations, and those "isolationists," as they came to be called, who wanted to take care only of American interests and clear out of Europe forever.

Hoover had advised Wilson not to go to Paris, but to send his secretary of state instead. "Your voice from the thunderous and free pulpit of the White House could be far more effective." But Wilson was so committed to his vision of a League of Nations that he could not trust anyone else to fight for it. During the peace negotiations, Hoover was in close contact with Wilson at Versailles, adding more hours of work to an already killing schedule.

Wilson's Fourteen Point program for peace was ignored except for one idea that took hold: the creation of a League of Nations that would hopefully stop future wars. But isolationists in the Senate voted against the United States joining the League. A bitterly disappointed Wilson suffered a stroke during a cross-country tour to win support for the League and later died a saddened and disillusioned man. Hoover, one observer commented, was the only one who emerged from the tense times negotiating the Versailles Peace Treaty with a reputation that shone even brighter than it had before.

Chapter **9**

"Turning Off the Lights"

Although Hoover was relieved to return to the United States after the Versailles Peace Treaty was signed, he did not find his country a happy place. Many Americans harbored ill-disguised contempt for Europe and its power plays that cost so many American boys their lives. Wilson, broken in health and spirit, had lost his will and authority. Like a national blight, racism, bigotry, and isolationism broke out in hot spots throughout the country. Washington sports fans cheered a U.S. sailor when he shot and killed a spectator who refused to stand for the singing of the national anthem.

Then Attorney General A. Mitchell Palmer's porch was bombed by an anarchist (one who is opposed to any form of authority). He reacted by ordering the compilation of 250,000 cards on radical Americans under the direction of 24-year-old J. Edgar Hoover (no relation), who would later become the first director of the Federal Bureau of Investigation. Palmer predicted that there would be a Communist uprising in the United States in 1919 and initiated a period of national red-baiting that cost innocent people their jobs and reputations.

Hoover despised Palmer's activities and was equally disturbed by the strikes and race riots. Despite his dislike of public speaking, as well as his fear of it (he confided to a friend that he was terrified every time he had to speak before an audience), he gave speeches throughout the country claiming that reactionaries "more subtle in their methods, more seductive in their platitudes, posed a greater danger to the republic than any ragtag band of radicals."

Resolved to live in the United States permanently, the Hoovers began building their dream home in Palo Alto on the campus of Hoover's beloved alma mater, Stanford University. Constructed of the most modern of building materials, reinforced concrete, the home was a unique combination of both Hopi and Algerian architecture and commanded a view of the East Bay Hills and Mt. Hamilton in the distance.

DELIVERING THE MESSAGE

But Hoover spent more time traveling on Pullman railroad cars than relaxing on the airy terraces of his new home. In cities all over the country, he called for a national program to conserve national resources, dig canals, and irrigate the earth, all under the enlightened guidance of good engineers. He supported labor unions, demanded better health care for children, and always called on fellow Americans to give service to their country. "Character," he said, "is made in the community as well as in the individual by assuming responsibilities, not by escape from them." He cautioned that precious individualism has to be tempered by free speech, equality of education, and voluntary organization for the public good.

Hoover for President

An admirer who had worked with Hoover when he was Food Administrator "nominated" him for President in a speech to a trade organization, and Democrats in California and Virginia started a string of "Make Hoover President" clubs. Hoover told them that he was not interested in running for President and also reminded them that he had been registered as a Republican since his 21st birthday.

Republicans, ignoring his claims of disinterest, put him on the first four ballots at the 1920 Republican National Convention. But many of the Old Guard (very conservative) Republicans considered him a dangerous radical because of his relief work and his support of Wilson's peace policies. They put their considerable weight toward a ticket consisting of Warren G. Harding for President and Calvin Coolidge for Vice-President.

Secretary of Commerce

When Harding was elected 29th President of the United States, he promptly offered Hoover a choice of Cabinet posts. It was in part Hoover's strong commitment to public service that led him to refuse a partnership with a leading mining company at $150,000 a year and accept the $15,000-a-year job as secretary of commerce, a position a predecessor had derided as involving nothing more than turning off the lights on the lighthouse and putting the fish to bed.

Hoover swung into action, organizing and developing the Commerce Department with the same dynamism and dedication he had brought to his relief missions. He divided his department into divisions and recruited the best experts he could find to head them. He directed his staff to gather all the information they could on their specialties and then publish pamphlets to make that information available to businessmen, farmers, and investors.

Concerned about the lives of working people, Hoover launched a year-long campaign to educate and pressure the steel industry into reducing the workday to eight instead of 12 hours. The steel barons were angered by Hoover and resisted his reforms, but utilizing the powerful method of disseminating information through the press, he asked his newspaper friends to write articles about Harding's desire to reduce the inhuman 74-hour workweek to 48. And he didn't stop there. He also convinced his engineering colleagues to make reports available that contained statistics proving that the eight-hour day was more productive than the 12-hour day. When the steel industrialists finally recognized that they were up against an adversary who was too strong and persistent, they initiated the shorter workweek.

Regulating Industry

World War I had triggered the development of a mind-boggling range of new products, from antifreeze and helium to drugs that cured malaria and typhoid fever. The universe was yielding some of its secrets to scientists such as Albert Einstein, Niels Bohr, and Max Planck. And new astronomical devices were providing astronomers with tools to probe the mysteries of the heavens far beyond anything man had yet seen.

Along with new products and new scientific theories came the development of new industries utilizing the new products and technologies. Hoover lost no time in stepping into the fray when those industries posed problems of regulation. With the development of commercial radio starting in 1920, the number of radio stations proliferated across the country and caused total chaos on the airwaves. Hoover called

The "Magic Box"

In 1921, a cook in Pelham, New York, put on earphones and listened for the first time to a newfangled invention called radio. His eyes widened as sound filled his ears. "This is a box full of magic!" he exclaimed. That same year, Secretary of Commerce Herbert Hoover described the radio as an instrument of beauty and learning.

By 1924 radio had begun to show its bleaker colors. The editor of *The New Republic* described the verbal and musical programs he heard over the air as "outrageous rubbish."

Hoover was to find radio both a godsend and a curse as he pursued his political career. In 1928 he and his Democratic presidential opponent, Alfred Smith, were the first politicians to make radio a vital part of their campaign. Hoover, who hated "stumping" the country selling himself, was able to stand in one place and reach an estimated 40 million people on election night. Radio helped him lessen the challenge of Smith, who was a charismatic platform speaker and loved to hit the campaign trail.

In the 1932 presidential campaign, Hoover had the disadvantage of having had the public overdosed by 95 of his dry, intellectual radio speeches during his presidency. Exercising poor political judgment, on election eve he delivered a scholarly, two-hour speech that monotonously listed the 12 points of his proposed program for America. Radio pollsters calculated that over 20 million bored voters switched to Franklin Delano Roosevelt that night.

Roosevelt was a radio natural. ''Each word, each phrase, each sentence, seemed to be built with the invisible audience in mind,'' one radio commentator observed. In a masterful move, on election eve Roosevelt sat comfortably at his fireside—his scottie, Falla, at his side—and spoke to his ''friends,'' giving birth to his famous ''fireside chats.'' Hoover, somberly standing in front of a microphone in his dark-blue suit and high, white collar, was clearly ''shut out'' by his opponent.

When one member of the Democratic campaign committee set out to discredit Hoover, he saturated the airwaves with the false image of a President who did nothing while the American people were going hungry and jobless. Hoover, unable to project warmth or sling mud in public, was powerless to counter this image, which persists to this day.

Ironically, Hoover was the first public man whom the radio—which he had called an instrument of beauty—helped to destroy. He would not be the last.

four national radio conferences at which guidelines for the new industry were formulated.

Still the idealist, Hoover hoped for voluntary self-regulation by the radio industry. When this proved impossible, he had to assign preferred broadcast frequencies. In doing so, he favored the big broadcasters because they were one of his main sources of information, a fact the small broadcasters pointed out with great bitterness. He also made a distinction between "unobtrusive publicity" and "unobtrusive advertising." In the process he dropped his advocacy of a complete ban on radio advertising and opened the way for the unlimited commercials that flood the airwaves today.

Eliminating Waste in Industry

With industry came waste. Hoover, an enemy of waste and a champion of efficiency since his early engineering days, created the Bureau of Standards to eliminate waste in industry. Working with over 900 trade associations and over 7,000 separate businesses, he instituted 86 major simplifications involving the standardization of automobile parts, building construction parts, and household items such as electrical fixtures, cans, and bottles. His department forged the path for the idea of interchangeable parts that made American products desirable at home and overseas.

Critics charged that Hoover was trying to get a whole nation to "ride in the same cars, wear the same kind of clothes, think the same thoughts." But he believed that standardization vastly improved the quality of people's lives and went ahead to promote uniform housing codes and zoning laws.

THE DEPRESSION OF 1921

In 1921 an economic depression (a severe decline in business) hit the country. Over five million people were thrown out of work as a result of the changeover from wartime to peacetime production and the consequent decrease in government spending.

Using methods he had employed in his war relief work,

Hoover set up offices wherever there was serious unemployment to dispense money raised in charity drives. He stepped up federal and local road-building and other public works projects, which provided thousands of jobs. He also instituted programs to repair deteriorating factories, which provided even more jobs. A real coup was setting up time-share jobs in factories so that more people could work at the same number of jobs. By 1922 the worst of the depression had been weathered. Indeed, business again began to boom and the "Roaring Twenties" were underway.

A Terrible Secret

Although Hoover managed to work well with Harding, he never thought Harding had the experience or intelligence needed to be an effective President. Hoover was also offended down to the roots of his Quaker soul at the all-night poker parties held in the White House with old Harding cronies he called the "Ohio Gang."

Hoover was surprised, therefore, when Harding invited him and Lou to go on an inspection tour of Alaska. They had been traveling for a few days when Harding summoned Hoover and asked him, "If you knew of a great scandal in our Administration, would you for the good of the country and the party expose it or would you bury it?"

Hoover's reply was immediate. "Publish it and at least get credit for integrity on your side." Harding would not tell Hoover any details of the scandal except that it involved the Department of Justice.

As they proceeded north to Alaska, Hoover noticed that Harding was looking more and more haggard. On the return journey, against the advice of his physician, Harding appeared at a stadium in Seattle, Washington, to address sixty thousand people on his views of Alaska. Hoover sat directly behind the President, and when Harding, half way through the speech, dropped some pages, Hoover picked them up and gave them to him. As he did so, the President fell against the podium and was rushed to a hospital.

After Harding died a week later in San Francisco, Hoover learned, as did a shocked and saddened nation, about the infamous Teapot Dome scandal. In addition to the attorney general, the scandal also involved Secretary of the Interior Albert B. Fall. Fall had secretly given certain private individuals leases to some naval oil reserves at Teapot Dome, Wyoming, receiving large sums of money in return. Those reserves had been set aside by Presidents Roosevelt, Taft, and Wilson for future use and had not even been allowed to be tapped during World War I.

Although Hoover could not say it was the scandal that killed Harding, he believed that it was certainly instrumental in his sudden death. "That," he said, "was the tragedy of the life of Warren Harding."

CONTINUING WITH COOLIDGE

Hoover was glad to continue on as secretary of commerce when Vice-President Calvin Coolidge stepped into the presidency. Under Coolidge, he established the American Child Health Association, which addressed the problems of poor health care for children, poor schooling, and poor child care in America. He also attacked the problem of child labor, asserting that children belonged in school in the daytime, in playgrounds in the afternoon, and in bed at night.

Hoover, always the engineer and always concerned with conserving natural resources, initiated plans and agreements to start construction on a dam which, when completed, would be the largest in the world. By harnessing the Colorado River,

*An avid fisherman since his boyhood, Hoover would seek a
break from work by fishing. He jokingly included fishing as one
of an American's inalienable rights.* (Herbert Hoover Presidential Library.)

which flowed from the mountains in Colorado to the Gulf of California, a region that was almost desert could be turned into fertile farmland that would encompass seven states.

An Ardent Fisherman

It was fortunate that Hoover was so ardent a fisherman that he would, on rare occasions, interrupt his demanding schedule to spend a few days fishing a favorite stream. "Fishing is for fun," he said, "and to wash your soul."

After irritable fits of anger caused by the tremendous pressures of his work, fishing would restore Hoover's equilibrium as well as his sense of humor. He added his own clause to the Bill of Rights by affirming that all men (and boys) are endowed with certain unalienable rights, including life, liberty, and the pursuit of fish.

Directing Flood Relief

In April of 1927, heavy rains and melting snows swelled tributaries of the Mississippi River, causing catastrophic flooding. Levees collapsed, sending water rushing on a 150-mile-wide and a 1,000-mile-long rampage, submerging towns and routing people by the thousands from their homes in Missouri, Arkansas, Mississippi, Illinois, and Kentucky. President Coolidge asked Hoover to take over the rescue work.

Hoover left Washington immediately and traveled to the stricken areas. He directed operations that removed 1,500,000 people from endangered homes and settled them in temporary tent towns complete with electricity, hospitals, kitchens, and sewers. The waters did not recede for three months. When it was thought to be safe for people to return to their homes, Hoover not only directed the logistics of that huge resettlement, he also furnished seed, animals, and furniture to help people put their lives together again.

THE MAN TO LEAD

During the relief operations, Hoover's good friend Will Irwin wrote:

> I saw him one May morning standing on the tottering Melville [Louisiana] levee, his airplanes scouting overhead, his mosquito fleet scurrying below, a group of prominent citizens about him listening to the wise, quick, terse directions that were bringing order out of chaos.

It was no wonder then, when Calvin Coolidge made the announcement on August 2, 1927, "I do not choose to run," that reporters descended on Hoover, insisting that he declare himself a candidate for the presidency. Many thousands of his countrymen joined the reporters in their request. To them Hoover represented the progressive and practical idealist who knew how to use technological know-how to improve the quality of their lives. He was the "Chief," who had, and could, accomplish near miracles. He was the man to lead the country into a brighter, more prosperous future.

But Herbert Hoover, again, needed time to think.

Chapter 10

The Magic
Wears Off

A merica was feeling good. Business was flourishing, and anyone who could work was able to find a job. Radio advertised a wonderland of new products, from automobiles to women's rayon hosiery. Money was easy. If people couldn't pay for all that went with the American dream, they bought on the installment plan (paid for over time).

WINNING THE NOMINATION

Hoover, after lengthy discussions with his sons and Lou, decided to seek the presidential nomination at the 1928 Republican National Convention to be held in Ohio. His popularity was high. The magnitude and success of his relief work had made him an international hero. As secretary of commerce, he had helped the country weather the 1921 depression and usher in an era of prosperity.

The Old Guard Republicans tried to stem the crescendo of support for Hoover by spreading petty rumors that he was not a party member in good standing because he had lived outside of the United States too long. They even stooped to the tactic of calling him Sir Herbert, implying that he was a British subject.

From their Washington home, the Hoovers learned that Bert won the nomination with an overwhelming majority, 837 votes out of 1072, on the first ballot. The second ballot made it unanimous.

The Democratic Opponent

The nominee of the Democratic Party was Governor Alfred E. Smith of New York. He and Hoover were alike in some ways, dramatically different in others. Both had come from poor families, and both were men of high character who would not engage in mud-slinging to win public office.

But two more different personalities would be hard to imagine. Al Smith, wearing a brown derby hat that had become his trademark and smoking a long cigar, loved social gatherings and was almost a caricature of the back-slapping politician. He was, in fact, a shrewd and energetic governor who knew the ins and outs of the political arena. He was also a staunch Roman Catholic, the first Catholic to run for President.

No Glad-Handing

Hoover, in his high, white collar, which critics would say symbolized his stiff personality, liked people around him, but could easily go from soup to dessert at a dinner party without uttering a word. He would not have been able to "glad-hand" a voter if his life depended on it.

Hoover refused to use a ghostwriter He composed his own campaign speeches, a taxing job because he was a slow writer and would revise his manuscripts seven or eight times. He spoke in a monotonous voice, looking at his copy instead

Alfred E. Smith, the Democratic nominee, on the presidential campaign trail in Chicago, 1928. (Library of Congress.)

of the audience. Al Smith, on the other hand, would lean comfortably on the podium, exchange jokes with the crowd, and speak without notes, his voice marked by a heavy New York accent.

THE ISSUES

Hoover and Smith agreed on several important issues. They were both for reform in child welfare, prisons, and business practices. Both ardently espoused conservation of natural resources and a more efficient organization of the federal government.

But when it came to a farm program, the two candidates parted ways. Smith favored fixing prices for produce and disposing of surpluses abroad. Hoover saw these measures as dangerous. They would bring federal control of the farmer's production and distribution, something to be avoided at all costs.

The candidates also disagreed on the controversial issue of prohibition. Al Smith campaigned vigorously for the repeal of the 18th Amendment, which had been added to the Constitution in 1920 to stop the manufacture, distribution, and sale of alcoholic beverages. Hoover never believed that prohibition was a matter to be dealt with in the Constitution. But since the amendment had been adopted, he felt obligated to uphold the Constitution, not find fault with it.

In the Mood for Magic

But issues were not the key factors in this campaign. Hoover was the "Great Engineer," the "Chief," the "Great Humanitarian." He was someone who, in his handling of the Mississippi River flood crisis, showed that his system based on "cooperative individualism" and volunteerism worked in peace as well as in war. He was the man Americans were bent on having as President.

In the "Roaring Twenties," as the period between 1920 and 1929 was called, when spending was high, life seemed made for pleasure. Colorful personalities—such as jazz greats Louis Armstrong and Paul Whiteman, writers Ernest Hemingway and F. Scott Fitzgerald, actors like the dashing Rudolph Valentino and Douglas Fairbanks, actresses like the glamorous Clara Bow and Gloria Swanson, adventurers like Charles Lindbergh and Amelia Earhart, and flamboyant gangsters like Al Capone—lit up the daily life of the American newspaper reader and radio listener.

Historian Joan Hoff Wilson has observed that for Hoover to capture the political limelight in such a bizarre and colorful period seemed unusual. "But by any criteria he was obviously the most active, the most vocal, and hence, perhaps by default, the most popular political leader." "We were in a mood for magic. We had summoned a great engineer to solve our problems for us," another writer observed, "and now we sat back comfortably and confidently to watch the problems being solved."

The Oversold Candidate

Hoover realized that he had been oversold by his publicity team as well as by the national media. This made him uneasy. Just before he was to move into the White House, he said to a newspaper editor that he feared the "exaggerated idea people have of me. They have a conviction that I'm a sort of superman, no problem is beyond my capacity. . . . If some unprecedented calamity should come upon the nation I would be sacrificed to the unreasoning disappointment of a people who expected too much."

When the final vote was tallied, Hoover had won a resounding victory, capturing 40 of the 48 states. Lou, Bert, and their two sons were at their Stanford campus home on election night. Even faithful alumnus Herbert Hoover might have tired of hearing a student crowd sing chorus after chorus of the Stanford song, "From the Foothills to the Bay," led by John Phillip Sousa. As the Hoovers walked out on their patio to wave to the crowds, airplanes dropped bombs that exploded red, white, and blue stars.

It was a great night for Hoover. He wanted to serve his country and enact reforms that would make it the greatest nation in the world. And the exploding stars told him that his country wanted him. How far he had traveled since boarding the train in West Branch, Iowa, as a frightened boy with two dimes in his pocket!

THE NEW PRESIDENT TAKES OVER

In the four months between November 4, 1928, and March 4, 1929, before he took office, Hoover selected his Cabinet, formulated administration policy, and took a six-week trip to Latin America in an attempt to improve relations between those 11 countries and the United States. Lou accompanied him and was of great help because she spoke fluent Spanish. The trip went well and laid the groundwork for the forging of a new "Good Neighbor Policy."

Inauguration day—March 4, 1929—was miserably cold and rainy in Washington. But the faithful and the curious and the admiring put up their umbrellas, buttoned their raincoats, and stood in the drenching rain as the new President rode in an open limousine to the White House after the inauguration ceremony at the Capitol. Among the well-wishers were old Stanford friends and men and women who had worked

During the Coolidge administration, children brought May baskets to the White House. Here, continuing the custom, they present a basket to the First Lady, Lou Henry Hoover. (Library of Congress.)

with him on his various relief missions. Lou, who had been devoting much of her time to the Girl Scouts, also had many co-workers there, cheering their friend on as she became the nation's First Lady.

Tackling the Problems

Hoover seethed with eagerness to get down to the business of running the country. His first eight months in office were a "whirlwind of reform." One of the first symbolic acts was to close the White House stables and to retire the presidential yacht. After one week in office, he stated publicly that "excessive fortunes are a menace to true liberty by the accumulation and inheritance of economic power." He announced an expansion of civil service protection for government workers, cancelled private oil leases held on government lands, and put James R. Garfield, a militant conservationist and the son of former President James A. Garfield, in charge of the newly created Commission on Conservation and Administration of the Public Domain. He formulated the Agricultural Marketing Act, which created an eight-member Federal Farm Board to "help farmers help themselves" by establishing marketing organizations. The act also set up a fund of one-half billion dollars that would stabilize farm prices by holding food surpluses off the market so they would not drive prices down.

Hoover allowed himself no more than five hours of sleep after an 18-hour day. And even then, it was likely that he was dreaming of what he would do when he woke up. His staff could not predict what directive he might issue in the morning, from beginning a five-billion dollar program to reform federal prisons to dismissing a commissioner of Indian Affairs long hated by native Americans and encouraging vocational training so Indians could learn skills and make a living.

The first mistake Hoover made as President, according to one "Hoover watcher," was giving in to a senator's demand to hold a special session of Congress on April 15, 1929, to consider increasing the tariff (tax) on imported farm goods. Hoover only wanted a slight increase, and advocated that the

Tariff Commission be given the power to make "flexible" tariff provisions that could change rates up to 50 percent. When the tariff was finally passed, however, it perverted Hoover's intentions by raising import duties up to 100 percent.

Disenchantment

Hoover had definitely been out-maneuvered on the crucial tariff issue. But he would never acknowledge that, just as he never acknowledged any failures in his engineering career (for example, pronouncing a mine in Australia to be promising that turned out to be a dud). When a friend criticized him for signing the tariff bill, Hoover evaded the issue by saying, "I'm afraid you'll have to give me up. I can never be the sort of man you want me to be."

Disenchantment with Hoover soon began to develop as some congressmen grew weary of what they considered his almost religious reliance on committees to "study" a problem. They also found him unresponsive when they called on him at the White House to talk over issues. As "Chief" of the Kalgoorlie mine, or of Belgian relief, or even of the Food Administration and Department of Commerce, Hoover led without listening and got away with it. But Congress was a whole different story. Congressmen expected to be listened to. As one senator said in disgust after a meeting with Hoover in which he claimed the President looked at the ceiling more than at him, "I think he's afraid we Senators will influence him, and he doesn't want to be influenced."

Disenchantment increased when Hoover refused to withdraw the Supreme Court nomination of a man whom both blacks and whites despised because of early statements avowing his white supremacist's conviction. He was dealt a humiliating defeat when the Senate refused to confirm the nomination.

While keeping up a frenetic pace carrying out his mandate for change, Hoover was worried about the amount of speculation, which he condemned as "crazy and dangerous," that was going on in the stock market. He was to find out all too painfully how crazy and dangerous that speculation really was on October 24, 1929, when the stock market crashed. Black Thursday, as it was called, saw stocks plunge, and with them the bold and cherished dreams of a "chief" whose image as a super-performer was crumbling fast.

Chapter 11
A Nation in Despair

What does it mean to say the stock market crashed? When a company wants to expand, it gets money to do so by selling shares of stock in its business on a stock exchange, such as the New York Stock Exchange, the largest in the country. If the company makes a profit, the stockholder is paid a dividend on each share of stock he owns. When many people want to buy a certain company's shares, the price of its shares goes up. When many people start selling its stocks, the price goes down. The activity of buying and selling stocks is what keeps the stock market moving up and down.

When Hoover took office in 1929, the stock market was making great upward leaps, followed by deep plunges. This worried him. Speculators, he said, dreaming of making a fortune quickly, were buying and selling "like crazy." The stock of General Electric Company, for example, had gone up from $128 a share to $396 a share in six months. And Montgomery Ward had skyrocketed to $406 a share from $132. In one day alone, eight million shares of stock were traded!

Schoolteachers, waitresses, policemen, and taxi drivers—the average, hardworking American who had never gambled in his or her life—had begun "dabbling" in the stock market. All hoped to be like the legendary beggar who had invested a couple of hundred dollars and made a quarter of a million.

THE "CRASH"

While he was secretary of commerce in President Coolidge's Cabinet, Hoover had warned investment bankers in 1925 that the "gambling fever" gripping the country was dangerous and asked them, in a spirit of voluntary cooperation, to control the speculation. But the bankers ignored him and went ahead with business as usual. When Hoover asked Coolidge to warn Americans against such wild speculation in the stock market, Coolidge responded that it was not the President's business to interfere.

In 1929, upon leaving office, Coolidge told the public that "shares are cheap at current prices." (Hoover had never liked Coolidge; now he hated him for his "shares are cheap" comment.) People borrowed money and paid for stock on the installment plan more feverishly than ever before. As President, Hoover had no authority to regulate the New York Stock Exchange. The only one with that power was Franklin D. Roosevelt, the governor of New York, and he chose to do nothing.

On Black Thursday, which dawned as an ordinary day, General Electric's stock plummeted $32 and Montgomery Ward's, $33. Fearful stockholders asked brokers to sell their stocks for whatever they could get for them. Desperate people withdrew life savings from banks to be able to pay the remainder of what they owed on their stocks so they could sell them.

Sixteen million dollars worth of stock were dumped in one day. By Monday prices were falling as fast as $15 a minute! Multimillionaires lost fortunes overnight. Some could not stand the pressure and jumped off the roofs of office buildings. Those "average" Americans who had taken a gamble on the stock market had their entire life's savings wiped out in the time it took them to eat a piece of toast. The nation reeled with shock, not being able to believe that this catastrophe was really happening.

THE GREAT DEPRESSION

The Great Crash, as it was called, has become the symbol of the Great Depression because it occurred at the onset of what turned out to be 10 terrible years of deprivation for millions of Americans. But most historians writing about the Great Depression (new books continue to be published every few years) generally agree that the role the stock market crash played in causing it is usually exaggerated. The economy was already shaky, not only in this country but in England, Germany, and France as well.

By 1930, depression was worldwide, with countries throughout Europe experiencing financial decline, serious unemployment, and diminishing prices for farm goods. When the United States reduced lending abroad and increased tariffs on imported goods, the already wobbly world economy collapsed completely. This in turn worsened the situation in the United States. Disaster bred disaster. Indeed, Hoover was to contend, true to his inability to admit failure with anything he was directing, that the economic collapse overseas is what caused the Great Depression, and that the problems did not come from within the United States.

Why?

The reasons for the Great Depression have been likened to the reasons why someone develops cancer. It is impossible to determine a single precise reason, though it is known that certain factors contribute to the situation.

Perhaps the most critical of the factors contributing to the cause of the Depression was the unequal distribution of wealth in the country. This was worsening daily, creating more and more people who could afford to buy fewer and fewer of the over abundance of products being manufactured. Businesses with a glut of inventory collapsed, jobs evaporated, sales in stores dried up, prices had to be reduced, which meant lower profits, resulting in even more lay-offs. It was a vicious cycle that no one could seem to break. Indeed, most historians agree that the cycle was finally broken only by the outbreak of World War II, a nasty way to bring about an economic recovery. But that seemed to be the reality for America.

"DAMN HOOVER"

There are many people who, to this day, believe that Herbert Hoover caused the Depression. The smear campaign ruthlessly begun by the Democrats in 1929 to discredit Hoover and set the stage for the election of a Democrat as President in 1932 was one of the most despicable episodes in American political history. The effects of that campaign are still being felt today. Whenever Hoover's name is mentioned, particularly among senior citizens, people not usually given to extreme opinions flatly condemn him as a cold, evil man who was personally responsible for the misery of millions of Americans.

A popular comedian's radio show at the time included this bit of dark humor: "There's a rise in the stock market," says one comic to another. "Oh," comes the answer, "is Hoover dead?" Another jibe had Hoover asking Secretary of the Treasury Andrew Mellon for a nickel with which to call a friend. "Here," Mellon answered, "take a dime and call all your friends." The humorist, Will Rogers, summed up the country's antagonism toward Hoover by commenting that if a man bit into an apple and found a worm, he'd say, "Damn Hoover!"

Reluctance to Admit Failure

Hoover's personality, which had served him so extraordinarily well during his 30-year career as an engineer and a public official, was ill-suited to cope with the peculiar circumstances the Depression laid on him. First of all, he was not used to failure. His method of handling it was to deny that it existed. Thirty days after Black Thursday, he predicted the end of the crisis in 60 days. "We have now passed the worst," he announced after 60 more days. "With continued unity of effort we shall rapidly recover."

One biographer wrote that as Hoover would not admit failure in business, neither would he admit failure in ideas. Once he had made a policy decision, he would not let facts or events change his views. Though he claimed that facts were what he needed to make anything work, he would sometimes reject those facts when they did not support his viewpoint.

HOOVER'S POLICIES, PLUS AND MINUS

This rigidity tainted Hoover's tenure as President. With banks failing all over the country, he would not relent and help struggling bankers with government loans. A principled man who believed that government intervention in business was bad for the country, Hoover held to those principles with the tenacity of a bulldog. He called a meeting of the nation's bankers and urged them to help themselves in the "American way." In 1931 they reluctantly formed the National Credit Corporation with $500 million to lend to threatened banks, but the scheme failed. That year alone, 2,300 banks went under.

In 1932, however, when pushed to the wall, Hoover finally signed into law the controversial Reconstruction Finance Corporation Act. This legislation created a federal agency with the power to lend money to banks, railroads, insurance companies, and state and local governments. Although criticized by the mayor of New York as being a "millionaire's dole," the act did decrease the number of bank failures in three months from 346 to 46 as well as rescue the nation's railroads from financial disaster.

Yet Hoover refused to give federal relief, a dole as it was called, to the unemployed. Speaking out of his ingrained belief that you must work for what you get, he contended that giving direct relief to the poor would demoralize them, that the American people were sturdy enough to take care of their own problems, and that "mutual self-help through voluntary giving" was the proper way, the American way, to deal with the economic crisis. "This is not an issue whether people shall go hungry and cold in the United States. It is solely a question of the best method by which hunger shall be prevented."

No "White Charger"

Such pronouncements branded Hoover as a callous individual who would help the banks but not hungry people. Hypersensitive to the angry charges beginning to rain down on him

Quaker Influence

The Quakers, a Christian movement that began around 1647, were first called "Friends of Truth." Later, they changed their name to the "Religious Society of Friends," its official designation to this day. The name "Quakers" was first given to the Friends by an English judge in 1650, because they were summoned by their leaders to tremble before the Lord. George Fox, the founder of the Quaker movement, reacting against the belief in witchcraft dominant in England, conceived of a democracy in which the Kindgom of God is within, an "Inner Light," that guides men and women along a moral path.

Herbert Hoover's belief in "cooperative individualism" stems largely, if not wholly, from his Quaker background. Holding a concept of religion that is individualistic to the core, the Quakers provided neither creed nor any head authority. Every man, woman, and child has the right to speak on any question at the Monthly Meetings, when members meet for worship and business. And every man, woman, and child is responsible for acting in a way that benefits their fellows and contributes to the unity of the group.

The Quakers follow certain practices which enable them to live with "integrity, kindness, helpfulness, simplicity, and individual responsibility." Hoover's speeches were full of expressions which supported the Quaker belief that moral and spiritual forces are the supreme forces in the life of man. In a speech in Kansas City before the Joint Republican Organizations, he cautioned that man's progress "is in proportion to the advancement of truth and justice." Morals, Hoover said, are what the American people learned at their mother's knee. They include "money and honesty, telling the truth, keeping one's word, fidelity to public trust, and helping those in need."

Certainly Hoover's unflagging humanitarian work, which continued to the time of his death, was fueled by his Quaker upbringing, as was his adherence to a principle no matter what the cost. This latter characteristic, which gave Hoover much of his strength, also made it difficult for him to change a course of action when it might be time to do so. Thus, he never did relent and give direct welfare to starving Americans during the Great Depression, a stance which in large part contributed to his dramatic fall from popularity.

Hoover, in his passion for peace, was a true Quaker, and he tried to live the kind of life his Quaker conscience dictated, a "life that takes away the occasion for all wars."

from the press and radio, Hoover did not revamp his by-now obsolete publicity machine to answer his critics. Instead, he withdrew more and more into the privacy of his storm-tossed life, giving fewer and fewer press conferences, making public very little of the good he was actually accomplishing in reforms and measures that were working.

Hoover's frustrated press secretary urged him to come

out against his critics and advertise his successes and personal acts of kindness (for example, he freed a father from prison for auto theft when the man's children came to the White House and told their story). Hoover responded that the public wanted to see the President on a "white charger of wrath with a flashing sword of slogans," and he was not about to oblige. The safety of a nation, he said, "lies in the determination of fact and policy and the patience in coordinating the minds of men for a common objective."

When Hoover finally consented to make a speech at Valley Forge in May of 1931, he called Valley Forge a symbol of the triumph of the American soul. "If those few thousand men endured that lone winter . . . what right do we have to be of little faith?"

A "Do-Nothing" President

Rather than inspiring the people, Hoover was sadly out of tune with the public, which infuriated Americans even more. By January 1931, over six million people were without jobs. Fathers out of work, seeing their children go to school hungry, did not want to hear about the nobility of privation and suffering. To make matters worse, the Democratic Party tossed another epithet into the public airwaves, calling Hoover the "do-nothing" President. A "do-nothing" President! To Hoover, a man to whom work was a religion, such a slur was deeply hurtful and embittering.

Shortly after the stock market crash in 1929, Hoover had used money that Congress made available for public works to build dams, bridges, highways, and harbors, creating over one million jobs. He began the construction of the Colorado River dam, for which he had done the groundwork while he was secretary of commerce. (Originally named Boulder Dam when it was completed in 1935, during Roosevelt's adminis-

Hoover Dam at twilight while under construction. (Library of Congress.)

tration, it was renamed the Hoover Dam in 1947 by President Harry S. Truman.)

Hoover also expanded existing national parks and monuments and created new ones, including the Great Smoky Mountains National Park in North Carolina and Tennessee, the Shenandoah National Park in Virginia, the Great Sand Dunes National Monument in Colorado, and Death Valley National Monument in California. In his four years in office, he built 360 public buildings and started 460 others, among them the Supreme Court Building and a five-story annex to the Library of Congress as well as buildings for the Departments of Commerce, Justice, Labor, and the Post Office — all in Washington, D.C.

But what Hoover did accomplish the public either did not know about or were in no mood to acknowledge. In December of 1931, Hoover asked Congress to create a Public Works Administration. However, Congress did not do so until Roosevelt's term, when it became a feather in Roosevelt's cap. Similarly, Hoover called for a Senate investigation of the people and practices involved in the running of the stock market. Again, nothing was done until Roosevelt took up the idea and created the Securities and Exchange Commission.

A Candidate Again

During the final years of his administration, Hoover's energies and spirit were taxed to the breaking point, though he would have been the last to admit it. He insisted that the attacks from the press did not disturb the "peace at the center" that, as a Quaker, he had worked to cultivate over the years.

Lou Hoover worked behind the scenes to make things as tranquil as possible, hiding the disagreements that cropped up within the official family. On the drive to a rustic retreat the Hoovers built on the Rapidan River, 109 miles from

Washington, Lou would work at being cheerful and try to rouse Bert from his dour moods. His frustration and growing hopelessness were causing him to retreat and become more and more distant from colleagues and friends.

Hoover, feeling the persecution of the press, the smear campaign of the Democratic Party, and the hostility of Congress, complained that he was being blamed for the Depression. The truth, as he saw it, was that he had done all that he could to avoid it, both as secretary of commerce and as President, with little cooperation from anyone.

Although he once commented that the presidency was a three-ring circus with a lot of bad actors, Hoover consented to throwing his hat into the ring once more for the presidential election of 1932. The Republican Party had no one else to put in his place. Moreover, Hoover still entertained a dim hope that if he did win the presidency again, there might be some small chance to bring the country to its feet, following a road he would engineer.

Chapter 12

"The Heart of a President"

The most unscrupulous of the "smear Hoover" tactics by the Democratic National Committee never came close to hurting Hoover as much as he hurt himself in the calamitous episode of the "Bonus Army." Several thousand veterans, most of them jobless, marched on Washington in early summer of 1932 to demand the passage of a bill that would give them their full wartime service bonus immediately instead of having to wait until 1944. Hoover was bitterly opposed to the bill, claiming that it was nothing more than a dole, and that paying the large amount of money that would be needed would put too heavy a drain on the national treasury.

Though his advisors and friends warned him that it would be political suicide to veto such a bill just before the election, Hoover retorted, "If Congress passes the bill, I'll veto it!" Rigid? Callous? Arrogant? These words weren't only on the lips of his Democratic foes; Hoover's own party members had begun to mutter them among themselves.

While thousands of members of the Bonus Army paraded up Pennsylvania Avenue, the House of Representatives passed

The Bonus Army, 7,000 strong, demonstrating at the Capitol in Washington, 1932. (Library of Congress.)

the Bonus Bill by the comfortable margin of 209 to 176. Hoover was in anguish. The veterans had set themselves up in camps where sanitary conditions were deplorable. He feared epidemics and an outbreak of violence. As the Senate took up the bill for consideration, tension in the city was the worst since the war. In a nightmare of bad timing, the Republican National Convention renominated Hoover on the same day the Senate began its deliberations on the Bonus Bill.

When the Senate defeated the Bonus Bill 62 to 18, the veterans shouted, threatened, marched, and held mass demonstrations on the steps of the Capitol. Appalled at the chaos, Hoover asked Congress to authorize $100,000 so the veterans could buy railroad tickets home. About 500 left each day, but a hard core of protestors camped out on the Capitol lawn, warding off the police with clubs.

BEDLAM ON PENNSYLVANIA AVENUE

Hoover could wait no longer. At the end of July he ordered his secretary of war to "use all humanity consistent with the due execution of the law" to clear Pennsylvania Avenue. He also ordered that women and children be singled out for every "kindness and consideration."

The secretary turned to General Douglas MacArthur, the Army Chief of Staff, to accomplish Hoover's order. Ignoring Hoover's instructions not to enter the Bonus Army's encampment, MacArthur did just that, using bayonets and tear gas and setting fire to the camps while thousands of horrified spectators watched.

Unaware of MacArthur's insubordination, Hoover released a statement in which he said he was "pleased," and called the action a victory for law and order.

"Well, Felix," said Franklin Delano Roosevelt, the Democratic candidate for president, to an advisor, as he heard the news of the fire, "This elects me."

Roosevelt was right. The public identified Hoover as the man who refused hungry veterans their bonus pay and then ordered Army troops to rout them from the Capitol. They blamed him for the fires and the death of a baby in the "eviction." And Hoover did nothing to inform the public that MacArthur had disobeyed his orders. For his own complex reasons, he let the blame fall on his own head. It was not until a Federal Bureau of Investigation agent who had been assigned to protect Hoover published his journals in 1966 that the actual facts were revealed.

Hoover further tightened the noose around his own neck when he accused many of the rebellious veterans of being Communists, a charge that was never proven by a Justice Department study he initiated. His credibility damaged even more, Hoover was now being called the man who ordered the murdering of veterans, although no veterans had been killed.

Swan's Song

Franklin Delano Roosevelt was a handsome man who had all the charm and social ease that Hoover lacked. In his acceptance of the Democratic presidential nomination for the 1932 election, Roosevelt coined the phrase "New Deal." "I pledge you, I pledge myself to a New Deal for the American people."

In 1931 there had been seven million people unemployed; by the end of 1932 there were 13 million people out of work. Roosevelt promised what Hoover would never give: direct federal aid to the unemployed and to farmers. He would set up public works programs which would furnish jobs for the unemployed. He would bring Americans back to a time of prosperity. In the election, Roosevelt defeated Hoover by seven million votes, carrying all but six of the 48 states.

On March 4, 1933, after the inaugural speech in which Roosevelt first used the oft-quoted phrase, "We have nothing to fear but fear itself," Hoover rose, quickly shook the new President's hand, and climbed into a car that took him to Union Station. Five thousand people had gathered to see him off to his new home, a 10-room apartment in the Waldorf-Astoria Hotel in New York City. "We won't forget you," someone called out as the train left the station. "We'll see you in 1936." Hoover, unsmiling, watched them from the platform of the train, holding his tall hat in his hand.

"I at least meant well," he had said in his farewell message to Congress. To a congressman's wife he later remarked, "No one knows the heart of a President." And to a close friend who was with him when the news of his shattering defeat at the polls had come in, he asked, sadly, "Why?"

Chapter 13

"He Has Endured"

Hoover had a special switchboard set up in his suite at the Waldorf-Astoria to connect him with Washington. He might as well have had the wires hooked up to Kalgoorlie. No calls came from the Roosevelt White House. Nor did any of the mail he spent $3,000 a month to open and answer yield the customary greeting from the White House to a former President on his birthday. Except for exchanged condolences on the death of family members, the Hoover-Roosevelt relationship was marked by an icy silence.

Hoover had to face the reality that he was not going to be consulted or even informed about what was going on in the executive branch of the government. This was painful for him, and he tried not to show his bitterness in public. In lieu of information coming to him directly from Capitol Hill, he subscribed to 30 newspapers delivered by air mail which he spent several hours reading each day.

ISOLATED FROM WORLD EVENTS

Though Hoover had rented the Waldorf suite because he wanted to be close to Washington, the freeze from the White House made it clear that he might as well go back to Palo

Alto with Lou. When he finally did so, he told reporters gathered in Oakland, California, to meet his train that he "believed he was entitled to a long, long rest." He had no plans, whatever, except to remain "silent on economic and political questions. Even on fishing I'm silent."

Lou was happy to be back at Stanford and to resume her work with the Girl Scout movement, to garden, and to host musicals illuminated by the 300 light bulbs concealed in the gold ceiling of their dining room.

Isolated from the heartbeat of world events, stubbornly sticking to his self-imposed silence, Hoover was, as a friend reported, "lonely beyond measure." The resentment he felt against Roosevelt and the New Deal burned within him, growing ever more venomous for not being aired. That Roosevelt's Cabinet and administrators as well as the press characterized Hoover as the fallen leader of a failed and obsolete regime chafed his very soul. Even catching a golden trout in a mountain stream could not remove the sting from that wound.

Congress, as responsive to Roosevelt as they had been resistant to Hoover, passed 15 bills within the first 100 days of FDR's term to get the New Deal rolling. Hoover saw many of the institutions and policies he had initiated changed in nature. The Reconstruction Finance Corporation, for example, became a gigantic federal bureaucracy that he was sure would advance the country toward socialism or, even worse, fascism.

A PARTY MAN

Hoover broke his self-imposed silence to campaign for Alf Landon, the Republicans' choice to run against Roosevelt in the 1936 presidential race. He was ready to let the arrows fly, accusing Roosevelt of intellectual dishonesty, of doctor-ing numbers, of "juggling the scoreboard" to prove that he had brought prosperity to the nation. Hoover appealed for the election of "honest gentlemen," Alf Landon and Frank Knox, his vice-presidential running mate. Roosevelt met these charges head on, claiming that in his administration the "forces of selfishness and lust and power met their match."

In a landslide vote, Alf Landon was demolished by an electorate that gave Roosevelt all but two states. Hoover called the defeat a mess and intimated that Landon had lost so badly because he was not a natural leader and the people always find that out.

Fighting the New Deal

Now that Hoover had come out of seclusion, he had tasted blood. He wanted to find a way to bring the country around to his philosophy of "cooperative individualism" and out of the entwining tentacles of what he regarded as the radical-ism of the New Deal.

Hoover began a campaign utilizing the techniques of pub-lic relations that he had employed so successfully in his re-lief work. He was now very much the loyal party man, something he had never been before 1933. Until then his al-liance with a political party was secondary to his private ca-reer and his role as a public servant. But now, in his passion to fight the New Deal, he became a Republican spokesman, pushing toward the "right" in his fear of what the Democratic "left" would bring to the country.

But as an avid anti-New Dealer, a faithful Republican, and the titular head of his party, Hoover was virtually power-less between 1932 and 1952. He was continually disappointed

in the candidates his party chose for the presidency. Nevertheless, he spoke for the Republican candidates in all presidential campaigns, though he was often regarded as more of a
nuisance than an aid, and publicly supported his party's policies. It was not until the election of Dwight Eisenhower as
President in 1952 that he felt good about his party's victory.
"The election," he said, "represented a turning in American
life from bad taste, corruption, communism, and to some extent, socialism."

BACK IN THE SADDLE

On a trip to Europe in 1938, Hoover visited many of the countries he had helped with his relief work, Germany among
them. After spending an unplanned hour with Adolph Hitler, Hoover reported that the man was more intelligent and
well-informed than he thought he would be, but that he was
"insane." Hoover also reported there was no doubt that
totalitarianism (complete state authority over all individuals)
was on the march in Europe. Upon his return to New York,
he condemned Hitler's treatment of the Jews.

Hoover believed strongly that the United States should
stay out of Europe's wars and let Germany and the Soviet
Union destroy each other. "One reason I have for opposing
wars," he said in a letter to the editor of *The New York Times,*
"is the necessity to adopt fascism to win wars."

Hoover raised nearly six million dollars for Polish and
Finnish relief after those countries had been invaded by Russia during World War II. He also established a National Committee on Food for the Small Democracies. In 1941 he
managed, through incredible persistence and belief in his task,

to get 37 senators to sign a petition supporting a relief plan for Europe. However, Winston Churchill, then Prime Minister of Britain, refused to cooperate and frustrated any of Hoover's further efforts.

Position on Issues

Hoover believed in adequately arming the country, but he also felt that arms should be limited "solely to repel aggression against the Western Hemisphere." Called an "isolationist" because of his adherence to non-intervention in the war raging in Europe, he nevertheless supported the war effort when the United States entered the conflict in 1941, confining his activities mainly to relief work.

In position papers he wrote after the war which, following his instructions, were not printed until after his death, Hoover stated his opposition both to demanding unconditional surrender from Japan and the use of the atomic bomb. He felt that both these measures would have been unnecessary if Britain, the United States, and China had offered Japan separate peace treaties.

The use of the atomic bomb, with "its indiscriminate killing of women and children revolts me," he wrote. "The only difference between this and poison gas is the fear of retaliation."

When it was suggested to Roosevelt that Hoover be asked to direct war relief, the President replied that he did not want to play God and resurrect the dead. President Truman, however, had no such reservations. An admirer of Hoover, he "resurrected" him, asking Hoover to take charge of postwar food relief. Hoover, at age 72, undertook a 39-country, 35,000-mile tour studying hunger in Europe and Asia and making

In 1948 Hoover visited war-torn Warsaw, Poland, on a tour of the countries he had helped as relief administrator during World War II. (Library of Congress.)

recommendations that brought the great famine of 1946 under control.

In 1950 Hoover decried U.S. intervention in Korea and favored the withdrawal of American troops from Europe. Though an avid anti-Communist, he warned Truman that war with the Russians would mean the extinction of Western civilization. He stated that he had "no patience with people who formulated policies in respect to other nations 'short of war.' They always lead to war. Our position should be to persuade, hold up our banner of what we thought was right and let it go at that."

Critics of Hoover recognized the soundness of his position by the end of the Vietnam War. They recommended, as he did, that the United States should lead by example. "You cannot slay ideas," Hoover said, in discouraging the use of military means to bring people around to the democratic way of thinking.

GOVERNMENT REFORMS

Appalled by the waste and inefficiency he saw in government during his presidency, Hoover did what he could to improve operations of and reduce spending by the federal bureaucracy. Years later, when Congress created a commission in 1947 to study the organization of the executive branch, Hoover was appointed its chairman, and the group was popularly called the Hoover Commission (the Commission on Organization of the Executive Branch of the Government was its official name). After many hearings and much research, the Hoover Commission made 270 recommendations to Congress, of which 70 percent were adopted, for reducing costs in the executive branch of government by eliminating duplication and waste.

Bert and Lou Hoover's carefully planned dream home on the campus of Stanford University in Palo Alto, California. Lovingly decorated by Lou, it was filled with artifacts collected by the Hoovers on their extensive travels. (Herbert Hoover Presidential Library.)

In 1953 Hoover headed up a second congressional commission with even greater powers to study and suggest ways to improve government operations. This time, after two years of work, the commission made 375 recommendations to Congress, and many of these were adopted. In 1954, for his many efforts on behalf of the U.S. government, Hoover was honored on his 80th birthday by a joint resolution of appreciation from Congress.

"HIS GOOD LADY"

Friends of Lou Hoover decided they would choose her as the person to be with in the middle of an earthquake. Hoover, in his fall from being the "Great Humanitarian" to being the man who was blamed with bringing on the misery of the Depression, experienced more than one emotional earthquake in the years following his election as President. It was his good fortune, however, that Lou was always there for him. She would smile encouragingly at the close of any speech he gave, send a telegram of congratulations if she could not be with him, or put her own work aside whenever she had to soothe, cheer, buffer, and sustain him. Hoover called her "his good lady."

In January of 1944, after attending a chamber music concert, Lou felt ill upon her return home and retired to her room. When he went to say good-night before leaving for a dinner engagement, Hoover found her lying on the floor, her heart barely beating. A few minutes later he returned to the living room, where his dinner companion was waiting for him. "She is gone," he said. How like Hoover to state in three simple words the loss of the one person in the world with whom he had shared the deepest, most secret, most sacred parts of himself.

FINAL YEARS

Hoover spent his final years writing and establishing the Hoover Institution on War, Revolution, and Peace on the campus of Stanford University. He also devoted enormous energy and love to the Boys Clubs of America, helping build up that organization from 140 clubs to more than 600 at the time of his death. "We have increased the number of boys per acre," Hoover said of the urban poor, whom he called his "pavement" boys. He strongly believed they needed a place to play, to learn a trade, to swim in a pool, "and steal nothing more harmful than first base."

When Hoover was 88 years old and in poor health, he made a last trip to West Branch to dedicate the Herbert Hoover Library and was greeted by 45,000 spectators suffering in the blistering heat of the August sun to honor him. In 1963, stunned and saddened by John Kennedy's assassination, though confined to a wheelchair, he sent a message to President Lyndon Johnson: "I am ready to serve in any capacity, from office boy up."

By the time Hoover reached his 90th birthday in 1964, 16 states had declared August 10 of that year as "Herbert Hoover Day." In a greeting to the American people on the occasion of that birthday, he said it was time for "Americans to take stock and to think good of themselves," a message not very different from one he had delivered many years before.

Hoover was now deaf and nearly blind. One evening his loyal friend Leo Strauss visited and read a mystery novel aloud to him. The next morning, on October 20, 1964, Hoover fell into a coma and died. His son, Herbert, Jr., announced to the country that the "rugged fight" was over. Walter Lippman, an eminent writer long critical of Hoover, was moved to write: "Hoover, in the field of war and peace, was always true to his real self, that of the bold philanthropist who binds up wounds and avoids inflicting them."

When the funeral cortege flew into Cedar Rapids, Iowa, thousands of people lined the 33-mile route from the airport to West Branch, where Hoover was laid to rest next to Lou in a gravesite on a small hill under some cypress trees. He had traveled a long and arduous journey and had now returned home. There were no military displays. The only sound was the wind stirring the cypress branches as a Quaker minister delivered a brief eulogy: "He had worked hard; he has been very brave; he has endured."

Bibliography

Burner, David. *A Public Life*. New York: Knopf, 1979. A vivid and well-rounded portrait of Herbert Hoover as a man devoted to his country who was then rejected by the people he desired to serve. The book is written clearly and with feeling.

Garraty, John A. *The Great Depression*. San Diego: Harcourt, Brace and Jovanovich, 1986. The author describes the events leading up to the Great Depression and the difficulties that Hoover had leading the country through those grim years.

Hinshaw, David. *Herbert Hoover, American Quaker*. New York: Farrar, Straus, 1950. This is a very personal account of Hoover's life by a close friend who is unashamedly biased. The book is valuable for the look it gives into the more homey details of Hoover's early life and colorful engineering career.

Hoover, Herbert. *Memoirs*. New York: McMillan, 1952. The four volumes of very personal memoirs were started by Hoover as a journal to share with his sons. Historians have found much of the factual material in them to be unreliable. Those readers interested in getting closer to Hoover, the man, will find much that is fascinating. He tends to be long-winded in these memoirs, just as he was in his presidential speeches.

Marquis, Helen Goldfarb. *Hopes and Ashes: The Birth of Modern Times*. New York: The Free Press, 1986. The chapters on the media are helpful in understanding the role Hoover played in the development of radio, as well as how modern media influenced the course of his political career.

McElvainie, Robert, S. *The Great Depression.* New York: Times Books, 1984. The author helps put Hoover's role in the Great Depression in perspective and seeks to show that the forces which overwhelmed the country were such that no President could have succeeded in avoiding that national catastrophe.

Smith, Richard Norton. *An Uncommon Man.* New York: Simon and Schuster, 1984. This book is a pleasure to read; it is written with style and gusto. The abundance of anecdotes and direct quotations from Hoover help make this lively and informative reading.

Wilson, Joan Hoff. *Herbert Hoover, Forotten Progressive.* Boston: Little Brown, 1975. Most young readers will find Professor Wilson's detailed account of Herbert Hoover's life and career too sophisticated to read from cover to cover. The first and last chapters, "The Quaker as Man of the World" and "The Quaker Out of Tune With the World," provide a good framework within which to fit Hoover's life as a public servant and as President.

Index

Australia, 28–29, 32, 43–44

Belgium, 51–56
Bewick, Moreing and Company, 28–29, 33, 42, 44
Bonus Army, 101
Bonus Bill, 102
Boulder Dam, 97
Boxer Rebellion, 38–40
Boxers, 38–40
Branner, John, 17–19, 24, 26, 31, 45, 63
Boys Clubs of America, 114

China, 33, 36, 39, 46
Commission for Relief in Belgium (CRB), 51, 53, 54, 55, 58
Coolgardie, Australia, 29, 31
Coolidge, Calvin, 69, 75, 77–78, 90
Churchill, Winston, 52–53, 109

Democratic Party, 80, 100–101
Department of Commerce, 69, 75
De re Metallica, 45

Eisenhower, Dwight D., 108
Empress Dowager, The (of China), 36, 38

Federal Farm Board, 86
Francis Ferdinand (Austrian Archduke), 47–48

Germany, 48, 50–52, 56, 63, 91, 108
George, Lloyd, 52
Great Depression, 90–98

"Gwalia, The Sons of," 32

Harding, Warren G., 69–70, 74–75
Harrison, Benjamin, 18
Hoover Dam, 98, 99
Hoover, Herbert C.,
    and the American Relief Committee, 49
    birth of, 8
    childhood of, 1–7
    college years of, 14–21, 22–26
    death of, 114
    as Food Administrator, 57–58, 69
    on fishing, 76–77
    and the Hoover Memorial Library, 114
    and the Hoover Institution on War, Revolution and Peace, 114
    physical appearance of, 15, 19, 25, 29
    renomination of for presidency in 1932, 100
    as Republican presidential candidate in 1928, 79
    marriage of, 34
    retirement of, 114–115
    as secretary of commerce, 69, 75, 99
Hoover, Huldah Minthorn (mother of Herbert Hoover), 1, 4, 8, 10, 12
Hoover, Jesse (father of Herbert Hoover), 3, 8
Hoover, Lou Henry (wife of Herbert Hoover), 23–26, 34–36, 38–44, 48–50, 53, 61, 64, 74, 79, 84–85, 100, 106, 113, 115

Hoover, Mary (May, sister of Herbert Hoover), 1, 6, 10, 21, 28
Hoover, Theodore (Tad, brother of Herbert Hoover), 1–2, 6, 10–12, 21, 28
"Hooverizing," 59, 61

Irwin, Will, 51, 65, 78

Janin, Louis, 27

Landon, Alfred, 106–107
League of Nations, 65–66
Lindgren, Waldemar, 19, 22, 27

MacArthur, General Douglas, 103
Minthorn, John Henry (uncle of Herbert Hoover), 1, 3, 4, 7–9, 11–12, 16

National Credit Corporation, 94
Newberry Academy, 9
Newberg, Oregon, 3, 6, 10, 16
"New Deal," 104, 106–107

Oregon Land Company, 12–13, 15

Palo Alto, California, 14, 57, 105
Prohibition, 82

Quakers, 3, 4, 6, 9, 12, 14, 34, 36, 40, 42, 47, 95–96, 99, 115

Radio, 70–71
Republican Party, 65, 69, 79
Roosevelt, Franklin Delano, 72, 103–104, 107

Salem, Oregon, 11–12, 16
Smith, Alfred E., 90
Smoot-Hawley Bill, 86–87
Stanford University, 15–16, 19, 23, 26, 51, 68, 84, 112
Stock market, 48, 88–89

Teapot Dome, 75
Tientsin, China, 34, 36, 40
Treaty of Versailles, 66–67
Truman, Harry S., 99, 109

United States Geologic Service, 19
United States Grain Corporation, 63

Waldorf-Astoria Hotel, 104
War Council, 63
West Branch, Iowa, 1, 4, 8, 57, 84, 114
Wilbur, Ray Lyman, 23
Wilson, Woodrow, 47, 56–57, 59, 61–62, 65–66, 69

Zimmermann, Arthur, 56